JAINISM
IN
THE NEW MILLENNIUM

JAINISM
IN
THE NEW MILLENNIUM

Ramjee Singh

Commonwealth

Jainism in the New Millennium

First Published : 2010

ISBN 978-81-311-0306-7

Published by :
COMMONWEALTH PUBLISHERS PVT. LTD.
4831/24, Prahlad Street,
Ansari Road, Darya Ganj,
New Delhi - 110002
Ph. : 23272541, 23257835
Fax : 91- 011- 23257835
e-mail : commonwealthbooks@gmail.com

Laser Typesetting by :
Dimple Computers
Delhi

Printed at :
Roshan Offset Printers
Delhi

Preface

Though myself a Hindu, I have great pleasure and privilege in presenting this work on 'Jainism as a World Religion'. To speak of beauty and grace of one's religion is good but to think of the splendour and grandeur of other's religion is the need of the hour. My second reason for presenting such a work is because Jainism has been a victim of many misunderstandings both in the West and the East. According to some scholars it has been derived from Buddhism or is a part of Hinduism. Perhaps they think that the whole of India is Hindu. No doubt, the Vedic and Hindu thought and culture have been the most dominant feature in India's religious and cultural life, it is also true that India has been the mother of at least four religions—Buddhism, Jainism, Sikhism and Hinduism with their numerous sects and sub-sects. Jainism is the sublimest gift of Indian culture not only to India but to the whole humanity. From the point of its historicity and antiquity, Jainism is one of the oldest religions of the earth and at least as old as Hinduism if not older because we find numerous references about the Jain Prophets in the most authentic scriptures of the Hindus. However, the relation between Hinduism and Jainism is the same as between children with different identities but clinging to their common parentage of Indian culture. Hinduism has been abundantly influenced by Jain ethics and style of life and so Jainism has also assimilated many important elements of the Hindu social ethos in their day to day life. Even in future, one cannot flourish and blossom without the other.

However, like every religion, Jainism has its own mission to the world—equality (Samata) and non-violence, which are more relevant today than ever before. Of course, non-violence is no monopoly of Jainism. Even the Hindu scriptures are full of the ideas about non-violence. Buddhism emphasises compassion, so Christianity lays stress upon "peace". Islam literally means 'peace'. But it was left to the Jains to formulate the ideological foundation of non-violence in all its aspects—word, deed and thought. According to the Jain scripture, "all our miseries arise from violence." (हिंसय्य सूयाई दुहाई, *Sutra Kratanga,* 1.10.21), therefore the best way is to look upon all living beings as our own. (आयातुले पयासु *Ibid.*, 1.11.3.) In accordance with this vision arises the idea of "universal friendliness" (मित्तिं भूएहि कप्पये *Ibid.*, 1.15.30.) This universalism in behaviour is the result of a faith that all life is bound together (परस्परो ग्रहो जीवानाम्) And when it speaks of life, it speaks of not only the human, animal but also of the vegetable life, nay even the material kingdom.

The greatness of the Jains lay in the fact that unlike some major religions like Buddhism, Islam and Christianity, it never had any interest in missionarising into practice or conceive the idea of prosetylising. To the Jains, religion is realisation, it is the inner nature that has reached in each man a certain stage of development and unfolding that can raise him to the status of perfect soul having four fold infinities (अनन्त चतुष्टय). Therefore evangelical spirit and missionary ambitions have been unknown to the Jains.

Much has been said of the common good of religious unity but so long we maintain even a lingering hope that this unity will be achieved by the triumph of any one of the religions and the condemnation and destruction of others, to them, we can gently but firmly say : "My dear brother and sister, this is worse than day-dreaming." Do I wish that the whole of the world should become Hindu, God forbid. Like the seed of the earth get sustenance from water, light and develops into a plant so also each should try to assimilate the spirit of others and yet preserve its individuality. To quote Swami Vivekananda :

> Holiness, purity and charity are not the exclusive possessions of any church in the world, and that every system has produced men and women of the most exalted

character. If anybody dreams of exclusive survival of his own religion and destruction of others, we should simply pity him from the bottom of our heart."

Absolutistic thinking is bad everywhere but is totally unacceptable in the realm of religion and spirituality. Nobody can claim to have the monopoly of truth hence to impose their own ideology and faith upon others is anti-religious and anti-spiritual. It is also negation of equality, love and non-violence. The Jains, true to their non-absolutistic heritage, have never come into conflict with other religious communities, although it has enriched, both materially and spiritually, the common heritage of India as well as of the whole of humanity.

Universalism is, therefore, ingrained in the Jain outlook in its action, in its nomenclature and in its primal key verse of its prayer. The term Jain implies a 'victor'. One who conquers his lust, anger, greed, pride etc. can safely call himself a Jain. Its basic prater is also universal and non-denominational. The Jain prayer requires us to salute and bow before the Ablest, the Perfect, the Perceptor, the Teacher and all the souls of the world. There is no mention of Jain or non-Jain, what to speck of distinguishing between Jain and non-Jain, they do not like to distinguish between the human beings, sub-human species, vegetable kingdom and the material world. Everything is filled with life. As our life is most dear to us, so life of others should be dear to us. Hence taking away life of others or even injuring them is an act of negation of life.

True, Jainism does not believe in a Creator God, but it denies God only to assert the dignity of man. It is religion of self-help and seeks to raise man to the status of divinity. In other words, though it denies the existence of God, it makes every individual divine, endowed with infinite faith, knowledge, power and bliss. It is thus the "religion of man" rather than the "religion of God".

The Earth Summit held at Rio (3-12th September 1992) and holding of the Centenary Parliament of the World's Religion (28th August to 4th September 1993) signify that the days of national chauvinism and religious fundamentalism are over. We have not only to think globally but also in a global spirit, not for any altruistic motive but for the sake of our very existence. Threat of a thermo-nuclear war has not been over, though somewhat receded. On the other hand, terrorism has assumed the form of an undeclared world war against humanity, perhaps more heinous and more cowardly. Religious fundamentalism has proved to be the greatest danger for human rights and creativity of man. Population explosion, especially in the Third World countries and the rape of the earth under the leadership of the developed nations, necessitated by a consumerist style of life, have posed an unprecedented ecological disaster.

Today, what is needed is not only a Parliament of Religions but Parliament of the Man. Religion is for man, not man for religion. If religions fail to bind us together and liberate mankind from sectarianism and superstition, hatred and violence, it is better to be irreligious and heretic.

When we think of religion today, it is mainly in terms of rites and rituals, sacraments and ceremonies, churches and evangelical missions. Universal ethics and spirituality seldom get as much prominence. In fact religion should be the inner nature of man which should reflect his moral fibre and spiritual trupir. Religion should project the spirit of man, it should not become his fetters. It is a blasphemy to regard Jesus, Buddha, Mohammad, etc., to be the exclusive patents of the Christians, the Buddhists or the Muslims respectively. What is the harm if the people of the whole world call themselves as Christians, if Christianity stands for crucification and purification of the spirit? But when Christianity is equated with Churchanity, we have a bloody Bosnia or the Middle East and then we need such an exercise as inter-faith dialogue or a Ministry of Reconciliation under the Vatican or a Parliament of World's Religions at Chicago. Religious separatism is as bad as Fascism or Nazism. Personal religion is like tribalism, if not worse. Hence, either we have a "Universal Religion" or no religion. If God cannot be Hindu, Muslim or Christian, how can we as

His children become different? If the human soul has no creed, caste, colour, race or sex, why should we have these labels? Why should we indulge in rival bigotry, fanaticism, and bitter hostilities? There is only one *Religion,* though *religions* are many. Religion is, no doubt, necessary to man but no particular church or sacrament is indispensable. There are two alternatives open to us—either we reject all religions or accept all religions. But both are impracticable. Hence, the only alternative is to inculcate in ourselves a spirit of Universal Religion or Religion of Man.

For one to think that his religion alone is right and the rest are in the clutches of the devil, is not only imperialism of thought and fanaticism but is also the source of hatred, animosity and violence. It is quite possible that there is truth in each of these religions. There might be different dimensions. Hence, the best way to avoid confrontation is to accept that the truth is manifold. Reality is complex and our knowledge is limited. Hence, it is safe to subscribe to the non-absolutistic frame of mind. Only such a non-absolutistic attitude in thinking can provide a strong ideological foundation for non-violence. Compassion is the moral basis of non-violence. Unity and existence of soul are its metaphysical basis but the Doctrine of Manifoldness of Truth and non-absolutism is the unfailing ideological foundation of non-violence. All dogmatism and fanaticism owe their genesis to this partiality of outlook and fondness for a particular line of thinking. The conflict becomes not only inevitable but also irreconcilable when the advocate of a particular religion develops a fanatic zeal and refuses to view it from other angles of vision. The Jains, in accordance with their philosophy of life, refuse to take an exclusivistic standpoint and thus try to overcome ideological and religious conflict. This catholicism of outlook is the natural outcome and extension of non-absolutistic attitude which may be regarded as a very strong foundation of a "world religion." There is no quarrel and conflict with the assertions and claims of Truth of the others, we have to appreciate their unique visions and assign their proper value in an impartial manner, in the light of its inter-connection with the entire reality.

As a corollary to this principle of non-absolutism in thought, we need a non-absolutistic principle in life. It cannot be anything other than non-violence and peace, which is also the demand of our survival. This doctrine of non-violence seems to have arisen out of a strong sense of the unity of the universe and a *reverence for life.* It follows that equal regard be paid to the welfare of every single man, woman and child, and equal, effective and maximum opportunities of self-realisation be placed within reach of all. In international affairs, the only alternative to non-violence is non-existence. In the social context, war and Machiavellian politics are not isolable phenomena. If disputes are settled on the plane of force, it is because our social life has been moving on the corresponding planes of hatred, frustration and exploitation. Therefore, non-violence is not utopian but most relevant to us. However, non-violence to be practical must aim at a wholesale transformation in the internal government of state as well as their mutual contacts to a revision of social and economic arrangements. All institutions require a virtue, a morality in harmony to function. Even science that violates the rhythm of nature are *satanic.* It needs universal human values like love, truth, non-violence compassion etc. The denial of non-violence (*ahimsa*) and violation of the rhythm of nature are equivalent to violation of truth. Society that seeks truth and is governed by the principle of *Ahimsa* to enable men to comprehend reality is its greatest richness. We must understand the power as well as limits of science. Science will suffer grievously and in the end reduce itself to a mockery if all its powers are not yoked to alleviate human suffering. But unless we learn to overcome and liquidate violence, the future is dark for all. On certain occasions, violence indeed appears useful. One can solve a problem quickly with force. But violence has a tendency to lead to counter-violence and counter-violence never ends. In the case of Cold War the principle of nuclear deterrence had helped promote stability, but did not create genuine peace. The last four and half decades in Europe have seen merely the absence of war, not real peace, but a facsimile founded on fear. Non-violence is not negative but positive. It is not only absence of war or bloodshed. It points to a wholesale transformation in the socio-economic structure as well as in the psyche. It is not something an abstraction or an ideal. It is a necessity. It is the very law of our life. It is the positive Cosmic Love. It arises from development of the mental attitude in which hatred is replaced by love. We cannot create so much as one particle of dust, therefore, what right do we have to destroy the very least form? True non-resistance is the one true resistance to evil. Good is all that serves life, evil is all that stifles. Good is reverence for life, evil is reverence for death. It narrows it down and cuts it into pieces. Hence, the best ethics consist of reverence for life. And this is non-violence. There is one religion—the religion of love. There is one message—the message of non-violence or Ahimsa, the message of holding one's own self in all beings. Militarism is not only anti-civilisation, it is also very expensive. Pursuing peace through military power places a tremendously wasteful burden on society. Total disarmament is, therefore, the only way out both for human survival and welfare.

Non-violence is not limited to the stoppage of war and bloodshed, it must also stop the arrogance of man towards nature. The materialistic civilisation has provided a life of luxury, consumerism and extravagance. We are faced with the cruel exploitation of natural resources meant for the coming generations. Hence, our luxurious life ultimately leads to the "rape of the earth". Hence either we adopt a life of plain and simple living or face ecological disaster, which will be more dreadful than the nuclear war. Non-violence is incomplete without voluntary curb on our extravagance. In fact, non-violence and simple living and limited possession go together. Jainism finds a pattern, a rhythm and a purpose in history. The progress of civilisation cannot be defined in terms of material progress but in terms of moral progress. "Rome suffered a moral fall when it attained high material affluence. So did Egypt and so perhaps most countries of which we have any historical record. The descendants and kinsmen of the royal and divine Krishna too fell when they were rolling in riches".

The Jains had foreseen these dangers and therefore, had emphasised the ideal of non-possession and the practice of voluntary limitation of wants.

The Twentieth century has been the century of science, the 21st century will be a century of the synthesis of science and spirituality. In Jainism, science and spirituality as well as non-violence and religion meet together.

The Chicago Declaration on Global Ethics as the basis of world religion also vindicates the claim of Jainism as a world religion. God, however great and good, He might be, cannot be the basis of a universal religion as there are religions like Buddhism, Jainism, Confucianism, etc. which do not accept the existence of a Creator God. Similarly, mythologies and rituals also cannot become the basis of a universal religion, as they not only differ from one religion to another, they do not constitute the true essence of religion. They are of secondary importance. The essence of religion consists in spirituality and morality. However, spirituality is a matter of faith and extremely internal and subjectivistic. It is based on one's intuitive experience. But morality is the basis of all our social, cultural and religious life. The first condition of a spiritual life is achievement of moral excellence. Jainism extols the virtue of character, apart from faith and knowledge. Morality is the matrix of Jain religion. Hence, it lays maximum emphasis upon putting ethical vows to practice. Gandhi also advocated "Ethical Religion" just to free religion from being identified with ritualism or mythologies. The five vows of Jainism—truth, non-violence, non-possession, non-stealing and celibacy, constitute the basic principles of social life as well as of "world religion." World religion is impossible without universal ethics. Jainism is, therefore, an ethical and spiritual religion, hence it serves as a model of 'world-religion.'

Ramjee Singh

Contents

1

The Jains and the Jainism

I. Jain and Jina

Literally 'Jain' or Jainism means a 'spiritual victor' (from the root *jin*) or a 'follower of a Jina'. Hence it has both a spiritual meaning and a class-name of a particular sect. The spiritual connotation is very high and charming. As 'Islam' means 'peace' or Hinduism means "one who is averse to violence" (Vinoba Bhave) and so on, Jainism is named not after an individual like Buddhism (Buddha), or *Zoroastrianism* (Zoroaster), Confucianism (Confucius), Taoism (Tao) or even Mohammedanism (Mohammad) or Christianity (Christ). It has a significant symbolic meaning that Jainism stands for "spiritual conquest" or "Conquest of Self". Real conquest is conquest over ones own unbriddled desires, envy, jealousy, anger, attachment etc.—the saddest of all failures is that of a soul. Life is the soul's nursery. Therefore, it is rightly said that it is our real failure even if we win the whole world but lose our soul. Jain teachers are therefore called Jina or Tirthankaras (Builders of the Ford) is not founder of the religion. He is rather propagator of truth and a path taught by all teachers in the same manner of his ever-present, imperishable tradition. Tirthankaras or the Builders of the Ford lead across the ocean of suffering. The term 'Jina' and 'Tirthankara' are equivalent terms. In modern usage, the term 'Jina' applies to any person who has attained omniscience, whether he goes on to fulfil the role of exalted teacher or not. However, in common parlance, there are many equivalent names and terms for 'Jain' like the *Rsabha-cult* (cult of *Rsabhadeva,* the first Tirthankara), Ahimsa-Dharma (the cult of non-violence), *Sramana* (Mendicant), *Yoga-Marg* (Path of Yoga), *Vratya, Arhat, Nirgrantha, Syadvada-Anekanta Mata, Saman, Bhavya, Saraka, Shravaka,* etc. However the term 'Jain' is the most popular one. *Jain* means a follower of *Jina,* which is a generic term applied to those persons who conquer the negative traits of their nature (passion, hatred and the like) and bring into prominence the most subline. Of such *Jina* those who become spiritual heads of the community are called *Arhats* (the deserving ones) or Tirthankaras (bridge-makers). One of the misunderstandings regarding the origin of Jainism is that Mahavira (the 24th and the last Tirthankara) is its founder. Though it is difficult to assign a date to the origin of Jainism it is a historical fact that Jainism is older than Mahavira. In fact, the Jains claim that their religion is eternal and during every *Yuga* (Era) it has been revealed by 24 Tirthankaras and Rsabha Deva is the first and Mahavira, the last Tirthankaras of the present age (yuga), who can be considered to be reformers and rejuvenators responsible for revitalizing and reinterpreting certain moral and religious principles when humanity began treading the unrighteous path.

II. The Jain Concept of History

In fact, the Jain concept of history follows from the philosophy of the world and reality. Jina Sena in *Adi Purana* (1.24-30) says that "history in the most general term is an account of past happening which must be authoritative, fruitful and righteous". Literally, the term Itihasa (history) means : "It so happened here". But it does not mean necessarily "the record of events", or a "mere chronicle of events". As Polybius, the Greek historian says, "If you take from history all explanations of cause, principle and motive, and of the adaptation of the means to the end, what is left is a mere panorama without being instructive and though it may please for the moment, it has no abiding value." According to the ancient Indian political scientist Kautilya history is equivalent to 'Dharmashastra' and, therefore, he considers the cultural factors beside the material factors as essential constituent of a historical concept. According to Dr. K.P. Jayaswal, "among the Hindus, the Jains alone have preserved a complete and admirable chronology for the two and a half thousand years or so after Mahavira's death". (*Jaina Sidhanta Bhaskara,* Ara, Vol. I, No. 4, p. 211). Dr. Buhler "an authority on Jain traditions, speaks very high of the authenticity of the Jain traditions and their value and importance of history (*Indian Sect of the Jainas,* pp. 21-73).

In the Jain canons, Rsabha, the first Tirthankara is believed to have lived for 84,00,000 years (Indian Antiquary, II, p. 261), the 22nd Tirthankara Nemi for 1000 years and 24th Tirthankara Mahavira for 72 year. (*Kalpa-Sutra,* 227, 182,168,147). There is a dialogue in which Mahavira is said to tell Skandak that "there is no time when the world did not exist", so Mahavira tells Jamali that "the wheel of history is also mobile." There are two motions, the symbol of world-order and progress : *(a)* Evolutionary-Progression (*Utasarpini*), *(b)* Involutionary-Regression (*Avasarpini*). In the involutionary period, there is gradual loss in the attributes of matters like colour, smell, taste, touch, tolerance, age, body and happiness. In the middle tier (*Madhyaloka*), all human activities take place. The worlds are arranged in countless (*asankhya*) concentric rings of land surrounding the central island (*dvipa*); each ring or circle is separated by water, much in the manner of coral reefs. The land of second ring from the centre of this system is divided into inner and outer halves by a range of huge mountains. The central island is called *Jambudvip,* after the Jambu tree which stands atop Mount Meru, at its very centre. Jambudvip contains seven continents (*varsas*) *: Bharat, Haimavat, Ramayak, Videh, Hari, Hiranyaka* and *Airavata.* (*Tattvariha Sutra* of Umaswami, III. 35). All these seven continents have been divided into realms : (1) Realm of Action (*Karma bhumi*) comprising Bharat, Airavata, Half of *Videha* (where *Moksa can be attained*) and (2) Realm of Enjoyment (*Bhoga-bhumi*) comprising the rest of four and half continents. The first ring surrounding *Jambudvip* is called *Dhatki-Khanda,* its land mass is twice as brom as Jambu : and has identical of continents and *bhumis.* Next is *Pushkarvara,* which is double the size of *Dhatki-Khanda.* Jinahood can only be attained in a *Karma-bhumi,* which are subject to an endless temporal cycle—half progressive and half-regressive (*Visarpani* and *Avasarpani*). They follow directly upon one another in unbroken succession; there is no period of dissolution (*Pralaya*) or demanifestation during which the *Karmabhumis* are not in one of the above stages. Then half-cycles, each last for a vast but finite number of years. The life expectancy of human beings dwelling in the *Karmabhumis* increases with each stage of *Utsarpini* and corresponding decrease with each stage of *Avasarpini.* It is only in the third and fourth stage of a high cycle, where there is neither extreme happiness nor unhappiness. Jain believe that there will be precisely 24 Tirthankaras, Jina, during each half-cycle. This is true for every *Karmabhumi* continent except the Videha, which is said to be always in a condition equivalent to the end of the third stage. At the present time, our earth (*Bharat-Kshetra*) is in a descending or regressive-half-cycle (*Avasarpini*). The first Tirthankar of this *Avasarpini* was *Rsabha-deva,* who is said to have introduced agriculture.

While the references of these legendary descriptions are found in original sources mainly *Anuyogadvar,* an important Jain scripture, we can also find its references in Schubring's *The Doctrine of the Jainas,* Winternitz's *A History of Indian Literature,* Vol. II, P.S. Jaini's *Jain Path of Purification,* R.L. Stevenson's *The Heart of Jainism, etc.*

There are plenty of scriptural and other references about the pre-historic existences of the Sraman-cult in Jain and other literature. Then there are words like Vat Rasana Muni, Vat-Rasana-Sraman, Kesi, Vratya and Arhan. We can find references about *Vat Rasana* in *Rg Veda* (XII 136.2), *Mauneya* (*Rg. Veda,* XII. 1363), *Vat-Rasana-Rishi in Taittiryanyaka,* II.7.1, *Kesi* (*Rg. Veda,* X.II. 136. 1), *Jambudvip Prajnapti-Vaksaskara* (11.65), *Tillyopapanatti* 4.230, *Tilloyasara,* 590, *Kesi* and *Brasabh* (Rg. Veda X.9.102.6; XV.1.1.1 *Sayana Bhasya*), *Vratya* (*Atharva* XV.1.1.1 Sayana-bhasya); *Atharva Veda,* XV.1.1.1; XV.1.3.1; XV.1.6.19; XV.2.3.1-2; XV.2.4.1-5; XV.2.6.1-10; *Arhan* (Rg. Veda, 1.24.190.1; II.4.33.15; V.2.28.4; VI.1.1.8; VI.2.19.11; X.12.166.1; *Asura* and *Arhat* (*Vishnu-Purana* III.17.18; *Padma Purana,*

Sristi Khanda, III. 170-413; *Matsya-Purana,* 24.13.49; Devi *Bhagvat-Purana*. IV.13.54-57; *Vishnu-Purana,* III. 18.12; III.18.13-14; 111.18. 8-19; *Asura* and *Vaidika Arya* (*Matsya-Purana,* 24.37; *Mahabharat,* Santi-Parva, 227.22; 227. 49-51; Vishnu Puran, III. 17.9; *Padma-Purana,* XIII.412.

All these references show that there is great antiquity of Jainism. Herman Jacobi has refuted the Buddhist derivative theory that Jainism is an offshoot of Buddhism. According to Prof. Rhys Davids the Jains have been an organised community all though the history of India even before the rise of Buddhism. S.C. Vidyabhusana regards Jainism as "one of the most ancient and noble religions" (*Jain Gazette,* 1914, p. 35). If India stands unique in the world for the spiritual and philosophical developments, no one will deny that the credit belongs to the Jainas, no less to the Brahmins and the Buddhists. Sir Sanmukham Chetty has all praise for Jainism. He says : "I personally believe that if only Jainism would have kept its hold firmly in India, we would perhaps have had a more united and certainly a greater India today." (*Jain Gazette,* 1943, pp. 83-85). According to Prof. Herman Jacobi, Jain scriptures refer to Magadh, etc. as contemporary to Mahavira. In Buddhist scriptures, Mahavira is referred to as Nigantha Nataputta and his death indicated at Pavapuri (*Majjhim Nikaya,* Pali Tripitake Series II, p. 254; S.B, E. Vol. XXII, p.xvv; Samyukta Nikaya (P.T.S.) IV. p. 398; *Anguttara Nikaya* etc. According to Buhler, Mahavira must have been a great man in his own way. From Buddhist accounts, in their cannonical works as well as other books, it may be seen that this rival (Mahavira) was a dangerous and influential one, and that even in Buddhist time his teachings had spread considerably. Hoernule says that like his great rival Buddha, Mahavira must have been an eminently impressive personality. According to B.C. Law, the Buddhist tradition, Mahavira was one of the more important of the six Tirthankaras (*Historical Gleanings,* pp. 21-22). Rhys Davids says that there are references to mutual conversions between the two sects (*Psalms of the Early Buddhists,* London, 1903). C.R. Jain says : "The origin of the creed of the Tirthankars that is Jainism, has been a source of speculation and error for the orientalists, who have advanced all sorts of hypotheses concerning its rise." (*Practical Path, Appendix, p. 174*)

There are ample references about the antiquity of Jainism even in old Buddhist works like the *Brahmajala Sutta* (*Digh Nikaya*) regarding *Jinas,* or *Jala Kaya, Leshyas.* So in *Majjhim-Nikaya,* there are references about three *dandas* of body, speech and mind of Jainas and also about the conception sin. In *Anguttara Nikaya,* there are references about the Jain conception of *Dikvrati, Upastha, Prosadh* so also about Jain conception of annihilation of Karma, old and new, in connection with the meeting of Prince Abhaya and Buddha. In *Mahavagga,* there is explicit mention the Jain doctrine of *Kriyavda,* so also about *Asava* (*Asrava*), and *Samvara.* B.C. Law (*Ency. of Religion and Ethics*), Vol. VII, p. 472) gives many other examples of such borrowings and adaptations by the Buddhists from Jainism.

Thus there are indirect evidences of importance and probable high antiquity of Jainism recorded by the Buddhists. They mention Jains as opponents, for example, older Nigantha Caityas of the Lichavis, Samanphala Sutta (*Digh Nikaya*) and of *Chaturyama dhamma* of Lord Parsvanath. Makkhali Gosala divides mankind into six classes—the third being the Nigantha sect of Jainism. Prof. Jacobi has most emphatically established the antiquity of Jainism over Buddhism. In the *Uttaradhyana Sutra,* the dialogue between Gautama and Kesi clearly proves it. Jacobir holds the view that "Jainism is an offshoot of Buddhism" as erroneous. He further says in one of his lectures : "My studies of Jainism made me reject the old theory and convinced that Jainism is entirely independent of Buddhism. The difference between the two philosophies seems so great that it precludes any idea of common origin." (*Jain Gazette,* 1914, p. 169). E.W. Hopken (*Religion of India,* p. 283) also thinks that The Niganthas were older than Mahavira and this sect preceded that of Buddhism." Prof. Rhys Davids leaves no doubt and says that "The Jainas have been an organised community all through the history of India from before the rise of Buddhism down to the present time." (*Buddhist India,* 1903; p. 318)

Historicity of the 23rd Tirthankara, namely Parsvanath (887-777 B.C.) has been accepted almost by consensus (*Cambridge History of India,* p. 153, *Encyclopedia of Religion and Ethics,* Hastings, Vol. VII, H.C. Roychaudhary, *Political History of Ancient India,* p. 47; *Jaina Sutras,* S.B.E. Vol. XV. Introduction; even *Dharmapada* mentions about Rsabha and Mahavira. Almost all modern scholars have no doubt about the greater antiquity of Jainism over Buddhism like Maxmuller, Cldenberg, Bendole, Monier Williams, W.W. Hunter, Harvey, Wheeler, R.G. Bhandarkar, K.P. Jayaswal, B.G. Tilak and many others. For example, Jacobi said : "Jainism is an original system, quite distinct and independent from all others." ("Jainism in Non-Jaina Literature", *Jain Gazette,* Feb. 1918, p. 87). To G.N. Jha also says Jainism is of an "independent origin". (*Jain Gazette,* 1921, p. 46.) Jainism is neither an offshoot of Buddhism, nor the Hindu dissenters (T.N. Sheshagiri Ayer, *Jain Gazette,* June 1922, p. 145). Jains have an origin and history long anterior to the Smritis. (*A.I.R. 1927,* Madras, p. 228, Justice Rangnekar of Bombay High Court *A.I.R. 1939,* Bombay, p. 377). A.N. Upadhyaya gives details about Rsabhdeva in the *Bhagwat Maha-Purana* (*Parmatma-Prakasa,* Introduction, p. 39). S.C. Vidyabhusan says that Jainism reaches back to the creation itself. Dr. Radhakrishnan says that *Yajurveda* refers three Tirthankaras—Rsabha, Ajitnath, and Aristenemi.

We can divide the Jain history broadly into five parts :

1. From the twin-life to Rsabha (Primeval Period).
2. From Ajit Nath to Muni Subrata—(Jain Ramayana Age).
3. Age of Aristenemi.
4. Age of Parsvanath.
5. Age of Mahavira.

But we shall start with the Legendary History of Jainism, according to which the world has no beginning nor any end.

Time, which is likened to a wheel with 12 spokes going round and round since the beginning, is divided into two : *(a)* Evolution-Progress (*Utsarpini*), *(b)* Involution-Regress (*Avasarpini*). The names of the age are—

1. **Susama-Susama**—4 crores of ocean years.
2. **Susma.**
3. **Susama-dusama.**
4. **Dusama-Susama**—One crore ocean years.
5. **Dusama**—42000 ordinary years.
6. **Dusama-dusama**—21000 ordinary years.

The time-wheel goes round and round in unbroken succession once from happiness to unhappiness and then, from unhappiness to Happiness. This is the cyclic order from Progress to Regress and then from regress to progress, or from evolution to involution and from involution to evolution. In the third period of both the cycles, Tirthankaras called Jina were born. So far the present period is concerned, we should note that the first four periods have passed and we are in the fifth period. Hence these will not see birth of any Tirthankara. The Nirvana of Rsabha occurred three years and 8/12 months before the end of the Third Age. The other 23 Tirthankars were born in the 4th Age. Mahavir, the last of the Tirthankara died three years and 8½ months before the beginning of the 5th Age which began in 527 B.C. (*Dusam-Kala*). Both *Utasarpini* and *Avasarpini* periods follow upon one another is unbroken succession. These half-cycles each take for a vast number of years. The life expectancy of human beings dwelling in the *Karmabhumis* increases in the *Utsarpini* and decreases in *Avasarpini*. It is only in the Third stage and the Fourth stages of a half cycles when there is neither the extremity of happiness nor unhappiness, can any one attain *Moksa*. At such a time are human being sufficiently shortlived and unhappy to understand impermanence and suffering, yet free from misery to conceive of and pursue Moksa. Jains believe that there will be 24 Jinas during each half-cycle.

During the primeval period (*Adi Yug*), the Jain legend has it that the Age of Twins (Yaugalik Yug)—corresponding to it the Vedic Age has the Age of Man (*Manvantar Yuga*)—which characterise the Age of Birth of man and the Age of Early Civilization. In fact, this was the Age of Early Civilization of man, where there was neither any development nor any religious duties (*Dharma*), literature and language, philosophy or thought. This was the Age of Enjoyment (*Bhog Yug*). There was no ruler or king. Two things marked the age, wealth and enjoyment (*Artha* and *Kama*). Kalpa-tree provided them things needed for them and they remained satisfied with that. The Twins while dying gave birth to another couple, which grew by sucking their thumb and they lived like husband and wife. As their life was a life of enjoyment, they were not needed to make any efforts. But later on Kalpa-tree began to shrink its munificence and quarrels started and fourteen Manus were born. People did not use animals nor they were needed, but from Seventh Manu, horse-riding started. In the beginning, parents died after giving birth to the children. The Twelfth Manu taught people to cross the rivers through bridge, boat etc. There was initially no crime, hence no system of punishment but when things became scare giving rise to a tendency to commit crime system of punishment started. First five Manus pronounced *Aakaro* (*Ha-oh*), next *Makara* (Ma-Do, *not do such*), *Kulkar* stage led to *Dhikar* or censure. Thus fourteen Manus started a system of social engineering. The 14th Manu was Nabhi Rai whose wife was Maru Devi. His son was Rsabha. In short, this was primitive family system (*Kulakara*). In every system of social philosophy, there is conception of an ideal society or the primordial society like Manu. Philosophers have differently conceived the state of nature. According to Hobbes, the state of nature was nasty, brutish, and short. Locke regarded the state as idyllic in the beginning which later spoiled. To Rousseau this was the State of idyllic happiness. Similarly, Plato in his Republic has also conceived of an ideal society. Thomas Moore also conceived of Utopia. Hence, the Jain concept of primordial state of society should also be taken in the light of such an idealistic Utopia.

III. Jain and Sramana

The first Tirthankara of the Jains Rsabha Deva, also regarded as the incarnation of Lord Vishnu, is the primeval Sramana from whom the Sraman culture is said to have originated. The term *Sramana* can be interpreted in four senses according to the etymological derivation—*Sraman, Samana, Samanas* and *Samana.* The Prakrit term "Samana" is equivalent to Sanskrit word *sramana* (*Taittirya Upanishad,* 2.7; *Brahadaranyaka* Upanishad., 4.3.22, *Srimad, Bhagavat Mahapuran,* 5 : 3; *Srimad Valmiki Ramayan,* 18; Panini's *Astadhyayi,* 24.30). In Vedic literature, 'Sramana' is used as synonym of *Sramana* of the Rsabha tradition. (*Mulachara,* 9.120; *Sutra Kratanga,* 2.1.15). Those who indulge in manual labour and austerity (srama) are called *Sramana.* While the Brahminic tradition has started around the idea of 'Brahman', the Sramana tradition has started round three fundamental concepts of Samya (equanimity), shaman (control of senses), and srama (dignity of labour). The term Brahman has two meanings—prayer and ritual and later on the persons who performed prayers or rituals were called Brahman. During the course of time, instead of through their deeds Brahmins came to be known and their status determined by birth and lineage. In contrast to this, the Sramana tradition does not subscribe to the hierachical social order based on birth. Thus there is the value of social equality ingrained in the Sraman tradition. There is also a fundamental difference with regard to the pathway to the final goal. The Sramana tradition treats the pleasures of the world or hereafter as undesirable (*Heya*) and extolls the value of salvation or spiritual uplift (*nihasreyas*). Thus they are constrained to observe such means as are helpful in achieving those high spiritual status. Hence, they accept the culture of non-violence instead of reckless animal slaughter in the name of Vedic rituals. We can, thus, observe an ideological difference in social and ontological standpoints of both these traditions. Patanjali in his interpretation of these two traditions magnifies a bit more when he compares them as eternally antagonistic like the snake and the goose (*Mahabhasya,* 2.4.9). However, history provides instances both ways—of conflict and cooperation. Hence Patanjali's statement of characterising both those traditions as eternally and inherently antagonistic is not about the individuals but about the class. There might be some individuals on both sides who are beyond sectarian enemity but we cannot deny that there has been differences in many of their respective metaphysical and moral, ceremonial and ritualistic positions. That is why, the great Jain philosopher Hemchandra, who came many centuries after Patanjali, also cites the opposition between the Brahmans and the Sramanas. (*Sidha Hema Subdanusasanam* 3.1.141). But it would be wrong to deny interaction and inter-influences between the two traditions. Let us consider some of the points :

There is hardly any difference between the two traditions on the problem of non-violence (Ahimsa) and 'universal welfare' (*Sarvabhutayhite arthah*) not withstanding the traditional emphasis upon animal sacrifice, the general acceptance of the principle of compassion and non-killings. Similarly, the Sramanic tradition accept the Guru-cult of the Brahman tradition, to a great extent. On the other hand, the Brahman-tradition has been greatly influenced by the *Nivratti dharma,* a world-negating ascetic way of life of the Sramana tradition. Apart from Ahimsa, a most fundamental feature of the Sramana-tradition is its consistence on the virtue of equanimity through traversing attachment and hatred (*Vitragata*). It means that by merely practising severe austerity and physical asceticism, self-purification is not possible. What is needed is to overcome the duality of attachment and aversion. This is the goal of spiritual life. Whether it is non-violence or practising austerities, if they cannot enable us to rise above our attachment and aversion, they are not of much consequence so far spiritual upliftment is concerned. Hence a Jina or conqueror is he who has overcome the usual attachment and aversion. This is the state of equanimity, called the state of steadfast wisdom (*Sthitaprajnata*) in the Gita. This equanimity or *Samya* or *Samayika* occupies the foremost place in the Jaina religious scripture. When the householder adopts religious life, he pledges in all humality and solemnity to observe *Samayika* or attitude of equanimity. It is so significant that the great scholar Jinabhadra Kshemasramana (7th A.D.) has written a special commentary called *Visesa-Ujakayak Bhasya* and has pointed out that equanimity is the root of faith, knowledge and conduct. (*Darsana, Jnana* and *Charitna*). In short, we can confidently say that the idea and spirit of equanimity of both the *Gita* and the *Acharanga* is the same. Of course, according to the different traditions and historical perspectives, the interpretations and consequent actions differ. While the Gita forbids Arjuna to accept the life of a alms-seeker recluse as a result of sentiment, the Acharanga Sutra would never advise to take up arms and bloodshed. (*Acharanga,* 1.5.3). To elucidate this point, we can cite the example of Bahubali who accepted the life of a alms-seeker recluse rather than to attack Bharat or to insist upon to give his due share of the kingdom. Gandhiji in developing the idea of equanimity based on the teachings of the *Gita* and *Acharanga* has put forth the doctrine of non-violent resistance against injustice. The Jain emphasis upon equanimity is similar to the idea of *Brahmacharya* in the Brahman tradition and *Brahma-vihar* and Maitri in the Buddhist tradition. This concept of equanimity of the Jains is of two kinds—ideological and practical. But the entire ideology and activities of Jains are centred on the idea of non-violence. What is not conducive to the furtherance of non-violence is not acceptable to the Jaina faith. No body can deny that all systems of thought and traditions have stressed upon the importance of non-violence in some measure but for the Jains accept non-violence as a matter of life and death. Non absolutism (*Anekanta*) in thought and Relativism in Speech (*Syadvada*) is extension of the principle of non-violence in thought and language. To think that "I alone am right and the rest are in the clutches of devils" is ideological fanaticism. To avoid this imperialism in thought, while Buddha developed the doctrine of Middle Path (Golden Mean), Jains have developed the seven-fold dialectics of Syadvada and Nyayavada (aspectal truth). Truth is complex and man is not omniscient. What he can know is only an aspect of truth, not the full truth. Hence, Non-absolutism is the recognition of realism, and never a refuge of realism, and never a refuge into scepticism or solipcism.

Broadly, we can classify three different fundamental view points in Indian philosophical thought and cultural history—(1) The Brahmana Attitude, (2) The Buddhist Attitude and (3) The Jaina attitude. The Brahmana or the Vedic-Upanishadic thought flowers into the philosophy of Absolutism of *Advaita Vedanta.* "The real is one, the learned call it by different names, Agni, Yama and Matrisvan". (Rgveda, 1.164.46). However, the general attitude is absolutistic crystallised into rigid doctrine of absolute monism. The Buddha's attitude was conscious of the absurdity of a priori metaphysical speculations moving in a vacuum. Abstract logic cannot meet the demands of real life. The Buddha following the Middle Path could steer clear between Eternalism and Nihilism. The Jains on the other hand developed a non-absolutistic attitude, which presupposes both completeness and realism. As told earlier, truth is so complex its entirety. Besides, there are obstructions due to desire (*raga*) and aversion (*dvesha*). Hence to be on the practical safe side, it is better to stick to a principle of epistemological relativism. This is similar to the attitude adopted by the Buddha who avoided extremes because the admission of anyone of the extremes would involve either nihilism or eternalism. While eternalism implies inherent perfection, nihilism implies its impossibility. In order to avoid these two undesired consequences, Buddha adopted the middle course and left these problems imexplained (*avyakta*). However, this is not agnosticism as he believed in realisation and asked the enquirer to realise for himself. Truth cannot be expressed in language. Buddha calls himself an analyist (*Vibhajyavadin*) (*Majjhim Nikaya, Sutra,* 99), so Mahavira designated as *Vibhajyvadin* in the ancient Jain scripture (*Sutra-Kratanga,* 1.14.22). It discards any absolutistic approach or extremist positions. Another name for this theory is non-absolutism (*Anekanta*). It is pleasant to find that except the Buddhist and the Jain, some other orthodox systems also do adopt this analytic and non-absolutistic approaches. For example, Vatsyayana, the renowned interpreter of the *Nyayasutra* of *Aksapada* has admitted the relevance of non-absolutistic approach (*Nyayasutra* with *Vatsyayana Bhasya,* II.1.15 and 16, *Yatha Darsanam Vibhag Vachanam*). In Yoga philosophy, specially in Tattva-Vaisharidi interpretation of *Yoga Sutra* (III. 13), one can obviously find approval of the non-absolutistic (*Anekant*) standpoint. Similarly, Kumarila, the great *Mimamsaka* in his *Shloka-Varttika* (*Ahnavada,* 29-30) has adopted the non-absolutistic approach.

Whatever might to be the philosophical positions, the sramana culture is at least as old as the Vedic one if not older. Even the three terms of *Sraman* (श्रमण), *Saman* (समण) and *Shaman* (शमन), which characterise the Sramana-culture have great antiquity. The term Saman (शमन) is said to have an Iranian origin. Its Sanskrit form Sraman (श्रमन) stands for the Jaina and Buddhist recluse. In Iranian language, *Sraman* has become 'Shaman' (शमन) which implies either worshipper of idols or temple. In China, this word has become as *Shaman* (शमन) and in Japan *Shamon* (शमोन). Among the Tung tribes of North Siberia, this word 'Shaman' means the priest or the physician. Among the Buriats and Yakuts, this word is used along with other words. Probably, 'Saman' (शमण) of India has become 'Saman' (शमन) in China and Siberia. Any way, both these words are synonymous. 'Shaman' is originally regarded as the religion of some special tribes of Asia such as Turks, Mangols, Finna and Tatars. Some scholars do not regard 'Shaman' as a specific religion. It simply signifies some religious rites and rituals, and some activities of primitive religion. 'Shaman' also means "one who knows" or a "state of emotional outburst" or some activities for controlling natural forces and human souls.

In short, the idea of Shaman finds different forms in different communities. We can describe the following characteristics of the Asian Shaman :

1. One is regarded as an expert who has communication

with the spiritual world. He or she has the power to cure diseases and has some special powers.

2. He or she can control the spirit and has communion with them.
3. There are occasional fights between two Shamans.
4. The Shamans during the state of emotional outburst use different martial musical instruments and uniforms.
5. There is no trace of the prophet or original imitator of *Shaman-dharma.*
6. A Shaman acquires his position, inheritance, education and training from his soul and experience.
7. A Shaman acts like a priest, physician, prophet, future teller.
8. Different countries have different kinds of Shaman as in North Siberia, Eskimos, American Red Indians, Indian Shaman of Eastern land, South America, Malaysia.

It shows the comprehensive and widespread nature of Shaman culture all over the world. But we are here concerned with Sraman-culture in India with particular reference to Buddhism and Jainism. We have seen that there are three stands of Indian culture—(1) Brahman (Vedic), (2) Sraman and (3) The Lokayat. Brahman culture moves round three important ideas—Equanimity (Samya), Control of senses (Shama) and Bread Labour (Shrama). Though modern Jainism inherits the tradition of Lord Mahavira about whose historical existence, there is no doubt, but after great research Herman Jacobi comes to the conclusion that "Parsva was a historical person, is now admitted by all as very probable" (*Sacred Books of the East,* Vol. XLV, Intr. pp. 21-33). Hence, it is very necessary to study the tradition of Lord Parsvanath. His legacy can be studied under three dimensions : (1) Evangelical organisation, (2) Ethical conduct, (3) Scripture. But we cannot ignore the legendary history of Jainism tracing its genesis from Rsabha Deva—who is said to be the first Shraman and incarnation of

Lord Vishnu. His religious order comprised the Sraman, Sramani (male+female priests), Sravaka and Sravikas (householders). In Puranas, the religious order of Lord Rsabha is designated as Arhut-dharma, which is called *Nirgrantha-dharma* during the times of Mahavira, who was also called Nigantha Nataputta. It is only during the 1st or 2nd centuries that it is called Jainism. In the ancient literature of the Jains, Sraman is variously called as Samana, Samyukta, Rshi, Muni, Sadhu, Vitraga, Anagara, Bhikshu, etc. However, the word Sraman seems to be the oldest one, which is evident even in the Vedic literature (*Taittiriya Upanishad, Brahad Upanishad.* IV.3.22; *Srimad Bhagwat,* V.3; *Valmiki Ramayana,* ca. 18; Panini's *Astadhyayi,* 24.30). The term *Sramana* has been used in four forms—Sraman, Samana, Samonas and samana, of which 'Samana' of Prakrit language seems to be the oldest, 'Sramana' in Sanskrit is its equivalent. According to the Jain scripture, those who undergo austerities and do physical labour are Sramana. (*Mulacharavriki,* 9.120). One who maintain equal treatment with all creatures is called *Samana* (*Prasana Vyakaran, 2, 5*). One who is free from desire and aversion, pious and with equanimity is Samana (*Sthaniya Niryukti*) and he who is always rooted in self-control, carefulness, meditation, yoga, tapas, etc. is called a *saman.* (Nulachara, 9/96). This proves that all the four names refer to *Sramana. Dharmapada* also supports it. (*Dharmapada,* Gatha, 264, 265, 388).

In ancient Jain scripture, there are five kinds of Sramana :

1. Nigantha—Lord Mahavira and his predecessors.
2. Sakka or Sangat—Followers of Lord Buddha.
3. Ajiva—Followers of the Ajivakas.
4. Tamas.
5. Gairika.

Jain Order : The Jain order (Saugh) comprises the raints (he or she) and the Householder (*Sravakas* + *Sravikas*). The first two are recluse who do not have a household while the third class is that of a householder. In an ideal order, we find an exemplary co-ordination between them for example, no sadhu (saint) would go for pilgrimage or otherwise without the permission of the Acharya. Only those who had a life of a recluse with real detachment from the world would be admitted to the sadhu-fold. These was a fixed code of conduct which consists of observance of daily routine of study, service to those who are not physically fit, and austerities. Unlike the Hindu society, a Jain-order does not prescribe an independent clan who would be sole incharge of conducting rituals and study and teaching of religious scriptures, with the result that the general householder remained almost cut off from religious education. The general householders, along with the sadhus or saints, took to the study of scriptures and practice of ethical disciplines. Sadhus or saints had no truck with polity which is very much evidenced by the fact that Jain radhus are forbidden according to their ten commandments to accept food from royal personages or royal court. Unlike the Hindu social tradition, no separate clavs like the priests or Brahmins are there to look after the religious rites and rituals and are the keepers of knowledge about religion. Therefore, all householders and saints have open access to the study of religious scriptures and are obliged to follow the rules of ethical conduct. In short, the householders are conscious enough to thwart any attempt on behalf of the saints and sadhus to usurp their. The Jain order has allowed many house-holder scholars to write commentaries on important religious scriptures. Similarly, the Jains have always accorded high status and respect to the women. The Jain widows enjoy better social and legal rights. We know that Jainism has also fought against the evils of casteism, hence persons of all the four *Varnas* can join the Jain order. *Sagar dharmamarga,* (Verse-22) says that even a sudhra can become a Jain if his conduct is pure. *Samanatabhadra* goes to the extent of treating the outcaste Chandala like the holy dirt provided he is equipped with right faith (*Samyak-darsana*) (*Ratna Karanda Sravachara,* 28). Jain order enjoins upon every Jain to treat his co-religionists with equal respect.

It is due to this spirit of catholicity, liberation and progressivism that Jainism is still alive and kicking where as Buddhism has become almost non-existent.

2

The Uniqueness of Jain Spirituality

When we look at this universe, many questions come to us : who created and who sustains, it? Where do we stand in this great structure and who governs our destinies—some outside force like God or is there any other set of rules called Fate? The most simplistic explanation is to rest with the concept of God, who is at once regarded not only as creator, preserver and destroyer but also all perfect *i.e.,* omniscient, omnipotent, omnipresent etc. Connected with such majestic concept of God, there is the doctrine of God's grace. The redemption of every individual lies in offering sincere repentance and prayers to be relieved of the sin. Those who are somewhat sophisticated in their explanation attribute the sustenance and control of our destinies to some outside divine force and so on.

The Jains need no such hypothesis. It conceived an autonomous universe and an autonomous self. When we transcend the limits of ordinary biological man, we come in contact with our pure personality which is called self (Atman or Jiva). This is the experience of pure spirituality or pure experience. This is the absolute concrete truth. Jainism conceives the whole universe as a great cosmic mechanism with its own structure and functions and also with its own "self-propelling force". It does not look outside but looks within and finds the truth that man is the master of his own destiny. All our pleasures and pains are result of our own actions, called karma. Our saviours or enemies not outside us.

But there is no caprice or irrationality in the universe of

karma. The Law of Karma works in the moral field just as the law of causation which works in the field of physical phenomenon. This law of moral causation is autonomous and independent and also supreme. Hence the Jains do not need a creator God or a Dispenser of fruits of one's action. It has faith in the capacity of the spirit in man—the spiritual creative force called the *Atman.* It can achieve the four-fold infinities—infinite faith, infinite knowledge, infinite power and infinite bliss (*ananta-chatustaya*). Thus the individual self is raised to an infinite temporal and spiritual height. We can raise the self to the status of the Supreme also in the Upanishadic-Vedantic philosophy of That Thou Art (*Tat tvam asi*). When the Self is raised to the status of the Supreme itself, it does not need anybody's grace. Hence, salvation of the self is not the gift of any capricious being but it is the direct result of our earnest effort and self-discipline. However, it will be unjust to designate Jainism as an atheist discipline. For this, we must distinguish between naive atheism and philosophical atheism. The former is the cult of materialism and the rejection of the reality of the spirit or self. In this sense Jainism cannot be branded as atheism. The philosophical atheism rejects the concept of a creator God. In this context, we know that even some of the most important orthodox vedic systems like the *Sankhya,* the *Mimamsakas* and even the *Advait Vedanta* denied the existence of God. Even in the Vaisesika and Nyaya system, God does not seem to be an integral part. But nevertheless, they believe in the spiritual order of the universe. Similarly, although Jainism does not accept the existence of a creator God, it has firm faith in the spirituality of self. By recognising both the self (*Jiva*) and matter (*Pudgala*) as twofold substances, Jainism steers clear of the two extremes of materialism and idealism. The problem of self is the most fundamental problem of Jain philosophy. Though this problem of self is not a new enterprise, the special points of the Jain view consists of substantiating the notion of self without blinking the loftiest mystical heights on the one hand and without condemning the unabstracted experience as sheer illusion on the other. The self is an ontologically underived fact subsisting independently of anything else. The experience of knowing, feeling and willing immediately proves the existence of self. Everyone is conscious of oneself. (*Sarvo hi atma astitavama—Sankar Bhasya on Brahma Sutra,* I.1.1). There is no proof that negates its existence because by negating it, we posit itself. Sankara using the dialectics says that the negator is the self. (*Ya eva nirakarta tadeva hi tasya svarupam; B.S.* (S.B.) II.3.1.7). Hence Acharya Kundakunda calls the existence of self as "a great objectivity". (*Pravachana Sara,* II.100). However, to the Jains, self is neither merely an immutable principle as advocated by Vedanta, Sankhya-yoga and the Nyaya-vaisesika, nor merely a momentarily transmutable series of psychical status as in Buddhism, but it is a synthesis of permanence and change. Hence the Jains recognise the self from two viewpoints to make a synthesis. From the transcendental view, the self is the unadulterated state of existence and from the empirical view, there is self which has been in a state of transmigration and corruption since an indeterminable past leading to origination, decay and permanence. The empirical self is potentially transcendental. There is metaphysical identity between the two status of the same self but the difference is also undeniable in respect of the potential attributes. The relation between the empirical self and the transcendental one is identity-cum-difference. Apart from the rational arguments and testimonies of the saints and scriptures, we can bring into the opinions of modern scientists. James Jeans, Arthur Eddington, Sir Oliver Lodge, Lord Calvin, etc. have found strong idealistic tendencies in modern physics. Some of the scientists refuse to accept consciousness as different from matter. They have found that without independent existence of consciousness, we cannot think of the embodied self. They do not regard consciousness merely as an epiphenomenon of matter, but as the medium of origination of consciousness.

Many problems of the present life such as the state of pleasure and pain from the period of incubation of the time of birth of a child can neither be attributed either to the child or to his or her parents. The child in mother's womb has no role to play towards his pleasures or pain. The parents cannot be attributed because how can an innocent child be made responsible for actions of his parents. On the other hand if we assume that the child enjoys or suffers without any cause or reason, we accept irrationality. All these and many other such questions cannot be explained without the hypothesis of rebirth. And rebirth can only be explained only when we admit the hypothesis of a permanent substance such as soul. Even the so-called agnostic Lord Buddha and modern German atheist thinker Neitzche admit of rebirth.

Jainism, therefore, regards Karma as the matrix of the universe and the ground man of individual's destiny and the mould in which anything and everything takes shape. Karma is generally regarded as the principle of determination of individual's destiny, his well-being and suffering. There are three reasons : first, the problem of individual happiness and suffering is not an isolated affair, because it is somehow related to the entire universe. The past karma puts a world before the individual which brings appropriate pleasure and pain to him. In short, karma determines both his heredity and environment. Secondly, even Time, Nature, Matter, etc. are not outside the scope of *karma* and they are merely the different expressions of working of the universal law of *karma.* Thirdly, *karma* is the principle of determination of the world. The variation in matter and time can only be ascribed to *karma* if we are to avoid the erroneous philosophical theories of Temporalism, Naturalism, Determinism, Accidentalism, Materialism, Scepticism, etc.

In an important sense, the science of karma has been described as science of spirituality, which aims at unfolding the real nature of spirit of self. This is self-knowledge or self-realisation. But to know the self if also to know that it is different from the non-self, with which it is in beginningless conjunction. Karma is the material basis of bondage and nescience of the soul. The beginningless relation between soul and non-soul is due to nescience (*mithyatva),* which is responsible for the worldly existence. This is determined by the nature, duration, intensity, and quantity of karmas. The self take matter in accordance with their non karmas because of self-possession (*Kasaya*). It is therefore clear that the science of karma is a necessary part of the science of spirituality. Unless we have a thorough knowledge of the karmas, we cannot know about the true nature of spirit or self. The knowledge of karma removes that false notion of identity between the body and the self, and so on and this is nothing other than the science of spirituality.

Jainism has a special interest in the philosophy of karma. While other systems or Indian philosophy generally limit themselves to the two-fold or three-fold divisions of karmas : *(a)* Those which have not yet begun to bear fruits (*anarabdha*); *(b)* those which have already begun to bear fruits like the present body (*arabdha*). The former (*anarabdha*) again can be subdivided into two classes accordingly as it has been accumulated from past lives (*sanchita* or *praktana*) or is being gathered in this life (*sanchiyamana*); or *vartamana* or *agami*). Howevers the Jains go much deeper and present an eightfold classification of karma spreading into 148 subdivisions. According to the law of karma, first a man attains the fruits of actions in accordance with the moral quality of those actions; secondly, the attainment of the fruits concerned is an automatic process. The law of karma is not itself a force, but a general statement based on facts that all actions of all kinds are followed by their appropriate effects and that the sequence between actions and their effects is invariable and inviolable. Like all laws of nature including the law of gravitation or law of natural causation, it is grounded on empirical facts, uncontradicted experience.

We are born into a world governed by the law of causation including the moral law of causation called karma. There is no caprice of a step-motherly nature and her blind, mechanical forces. In the life of man as a spiritual being, we find three phases or aspects namely desire, thought and will. The character of a man is the accumulated effect of his thoughts as expressed in deeds. Just as it is the case with a man's thoughts and desire so it is his will and acts. We are effects of the infinite past, that the child is ushered into the world, not as something flashing from the hands of nature but he has the burden of an infinite past, for good or evil he comes to work out his own past deeds. We, and we, and none else, are responsible for what we suffer. We are the effects, and we are the causes. Each one of us is the matter of his own fate thus the law of Karma knocks on the head at once all doctrines of predestination and fate. Those who also believe in the existence of God and the law of karma admit the law of karma as autonomous that works independently of the will of God. They hold that the origin and order of the world may be explained by the law of karma without the supposition of a creator God. But it does not militate against the doctrine of free will in man. They bind us in a sense no doubt, but that is just in the same sense in which old habits of action put certain limitations on our present actions. Just as it is quite possible, though difficult for us to uproot old habits of action, so it is possible to alter and avert the consequences of our past deeds through spiritual *sadhana.*

The law of karma in its different aspects may be regarded as the law of conservation of moral values, merits and demerits of actions. Nothing befalls a man except as the result of his own actions and nothing merited by a man by his actions is lost unto him. As 'religion' is said to be 'faith in the conservation of value' (Harold hoffding : *The Philosophy of Religion,* pp. 6-12), the law of Karma may be defined as faith in an eternal moral order that inspires hope and confidence in man and makes him the master of his own destiny. The human will stands beyond all circumstances. Before it, the strong, gigantic, infinite will and freedom in man, all the powers, even of nature, must bow down succumb and become its servants.

Not only the modern man in the search of a soul, the first requisite for any philosophical adventure is the recognition of the idea of the self. This is the spiritual basis of our ethical life which can be traced in the endeavour of man to find out ways and means by which he could become happy. Hence, Alexis Carrel has dwelt upon the "Science of Man" in his famous book,

Man, the Unknown. The Jains subscribe to the doctrine of constitutional freedom of the soul and its potential fourfold infinities meaning thereby that the soul is intrinsically pure and innately perfect. But the soul and Karma stand to each other in the relation of beginningless conjunction. The soul by its commerce with the outer world becomes literally penetrated with the particles of subject-matter. The karmic-matter mixes with the soul as milk mixes with water. Thus formless karma is affected by the karma with form as consciousness is affected by drink or medicine. Logically, the cause is non-different from the effect. The effect is physical—Hence the cause (karma) has indeed a physical form. But unless karma is associated with the Jiva (soul) it cannot produce any effect because karma is only an instrumental cause; it is the soul which is the essential cause of all experiences. This explains the theory of the soul as the possessor of karma. A question may arise as to how the conscious soul is associated with unconscious matter? The Jains reply that the karma is a substantive force or matter in a subtle form, which fills all cosmic space. It is due to karma that the soul acquires the conditions of nescience or ignorance. The relation between soul and non-soul is beginningless, and is due to nescience or *avidya,* which is responsible for worldly existence or bondage. The soul takes matter in accordance with its own karmas and passions. This is our bondage, the causes of which are delusion, lack of control, inadvertence, passions, and vibrations.

Moksa or liberation is the total deliverance of the soul from the karmic-veil or karmic-matter. Influx of karmic-matter into the soul is caused by the actions of the body, speech and mind. Hence, what is necessary precondition of salvation is not only stoppage of the fresh-flow of karmic matter, but also dissipation of the old one through austerities. Then only the soul experiences eternal bliss. However, there is a dilemma : if *Moksa* or liberation is the product of spiritual *sadhana,* it is non-eternal and if it is not such a product, it is either constitutional or inherent or at least impossible of attainment. Even the Jain doctrine of constitutional freedom of the soul and the four infinities presents a difficult proposition. If the self is inherently good and perfect, how can karma be associated with the soul? If karma is said to be the cause of bondage and bondage the cause of karma, then there is the fallacy of circularity and also regress infinitum. If the karma is beginningless, then how can the soul be essentially perfect? Thus, all the doctrines of salvation and its means become quite meaningless. Hence, logic will force the Jains to make a distinction between the manifest and unmanifest. Liberation is not the attainment of what is already attained but manifestation of what was latent in the soul. In this sense, liberation in Jainism is not something new but a rediscovery of man himself through self-realisation. True happiness, thus, lies within.

The soul has, no doubt, inherent capacity for emancipation but this capacity remains dormant unless it gets an opportunity for expression, through some spiritual exertion through 14 stages of spiritual evolution. Here mysticism and metaphysics co-mingle. We can broadly classify these 14 stages of spiritual advancement under the following heads :

(1) Dark period of self prior to its awakening.

(2) Awakening of the self and fall from awakening.

(3) Purgation.

(4) Illumination.

(5) Dark period post-illumination and

(6) Transcendental life.

The dark period of self prior to awakening is a period of discontent and disquiesh, due to deluding karma. This is *Mithyatva* which is responsible for turning our perspective to such an illegitimate direction that in effect ensures perverted belief or non-belief in ultimate values. It is also corruption of knowledge and conduct as well. The plight of self is like an eclipsed moon or completely clouded sky. It is a stage of spiritual slumber with the peculiarity that the self itself is not cognisant of its drowsy state. It aims at moral-intellectual and spiritual conversion. Mere intellectual enlightenment is not enough. So also more moral life is not enough. What is required is tripple transformation in mental, moral as well as spiritual life. Intellectual attainments and moral achievements are unequivocally fraught with social utility, but morality pervaded with spiritualism can alone lead us to the transcendental heights. Right Faith (*Samyagdarsana*) is origination of spiritual conversion or awakening of the self (*Aviratsamyakdristi Gunasthan*), which is sometime consequent upon the instruction of those who have realised the divine within themselves or on the path of realisation through instruction from the spiritual teacher (Sad-Guru)—*Arahanta* (Bodily liberated), *Siddha* (Disembodied liberated), *Acharya* (Spiritual Initiator), *Upadhyaya* (Teacher) and *Sadhus* (Saints). There are types of spiritual conversion and there are requisites of mystic's journey after spiritual conversion. Then at the stage of purgation, the aspirant achieves a mental attitude of self-denial and self-control. Scriptural study is also necessary to develop right knowledge. Then devotion is also required which implies the sublime affection, circumscribed by immaculacy of thought and emotion towards the divinity-realised souls. Then there are 16 kinds of reflections as the embodiment of knowledge, action and devotion. After purgation, there are higher stages of advancement with the rise of Samjvalana and nine sub-types of passion in such a mild form that it cannot generate Pramada in the constitution of the self. Onward 7th stage of the 12th stages of spiritual development are meditational stages or the stages of illumination and ecstacy. The spiritual aspirant who possesses the fresh fruits of contemplation may encounter his outright purification, and expend a swing-back into darkness. This divides the first mystic life (illuminative way) to the second mystic life (transcendental life), where the slumbering and unawakened soul, after passing through the stages of spiritual conversion, moral and intellectual preparation, arrives at a sublime destination by ascending the rungs of meditational ladder. Now by virtue of this metamorphosis into transcendental self it neither abandons nor adopts anything, but rests in eternal peace and tranquility. The self which was once swayed by perversion, non-abstinence, spiritual inertia and other types of passions and quasi-passions refuses to be deflected by them. It is an example of divine life on earth. Potentiality has been turned into actuality. The discrepancy between belief and living has vanished. It is the final consumation of spiritual life (*Saryoga Kevali Gunasthana*). The next and the final stage is that of disembodied liberated stage (*Ayoga Kevali Gunasthan*), where the soul annuls even the vibratory activities. At both these states, the self is called *Arahanta* having seven kinds differing in certain outward circumstances. The *Arahanta* is the ideal saint, the supreme spiritual teacher and the divinity-realised soul, and established in truth in all direction. He is freed from anger, pride, deceit, greed, attachment, hatred, delusion, animal existence and pain. He has a life of super-moralism but not of a moralism. He is the overplus surpassing all that can be clearly understood and appraised. In eternal divinity, there is no devotional control of breath, no object of meditation, no mystical diagram, no miraculous spell, and no charmed circle.

However, the transcendental life par-excellence (Siddhahood) immediately follows the final emancipation and is in the disembodied state. This state of self is beyond even *Gunasthanas.* It transcends the realm of cause and effect. It is without body, without resurrection, without contact of matter, he is neither masculine nor feminine nor neuter. Its essence is without form, there is no condition of the unconditioned. Hence it is the termination of the spiritual adventure.

CONCLUSION

The uniqueness of Jain spirituality lies in more than one sense. It is integral as it combines the empirical with the transcendental, intellectual with devotional; faith with knowledge and conduct. Secondly, its supermoralism does not conflict with the highest virtuous life. Thus, it reconciles the life of spirit with the life of virtues, individual perfection with social goodness unlike the Platonic contemplation or Aristotle's theories. In fact, Jainism treats life as a unity in which the empirical and the transcendental are not treated as watertight compartments. Even in the Jain enumeration and classification of cardinal virtues, we find mention of spiritual conversion, scriptural study, meditation and devotion also. It is not fair to criticise to say that the Jaina list does not include the other regarding virtues of benevolence, succour, and social service because in the comprehensive list provided by Professor R.D. Ranade there is three fold division of virtues—individual, social and spiritual, which are found in Jain scriptures also. The Jain saint adheres to the observance of not only five great vows but is also an example of the dedication of his integral energies to the cessation and shedding of Karmas and subjugating 22 kinds of Parisahas and the practice of 12 kinds of austerities. Of the six kinds of internal austerities, Dhyana (meditation) is one supreme consideration. All the disciplinary practices form an integral constituent of right conduct. But the most important contribution of Jainism is to provide a practical guidance for the attainment of transcendental life through Gunasthanas.

3

What is Living and What is Dead in Jainism?

According to a proverb, anything which does not grow, dies. But this is a riddle that the Jains, as a religious community, have neither been dead nor have grown. From the point of view of its historicity, Jainism is one of "the oldest religions of the earth and at least as old as Hinduism if not older." Prof. Hermon Jacobi has successfully refuted the Buddhist derivation theory.[1] According to S.C. Vidyabhushan, Jainism dates back to the creation itself. He asserts, "Jain philosophy is much anterior to Vedanta and other systems."[2] To Hoernle, it is not difficult to prove that Jainism, far from being an offshot of Buddhism or Brahminism, was one of the earliest home religions of India.[3] The very fact that Vedas and other branches of Vedic literature make a mention of the name of *Rsabha*,[4] the first Thirthankara of the Jains, suggests that the Jain cult had been in existence prior to the Vedas. Rsabhadeva is verily regarded as the 9th incarnation of Lord Vishnu according to the *Bhagwata Purana*.[5]

The discovery of the pre-historic Indus Valley civilization of Mohanjodaro and Harappa throws a new light on the antiquity of Jainism. With its cult of nudity and yoga, the worship of the bull and other symbols, it has resemblances to Jainism, and, therefore, the Indus civilization is supposed to be non-Aryan or of non-Vedic Aryan origin.[6] Even Ahimsa, which forms the core of Jainism, is a philosophy which comes from pre-Aryan days and it seems to be an indigenous product of ancient schools of Indian thought.[8] The very fact that the great Hindu saints, who wanted to revive Hinduism in South India, had to resort even to persecutions of the Jains. This is a proof that Jainism must have had its hold on the people of South India. What was called *Manava-dharma* or *Magga* during the Indus Valley days is the *Rsabha-cult* or *Jaindharama; Vratya* religion in the Vedic age; *Ahimsa-dharma* or *Atmadharma* during the Upanishads, during Buddha's times as *Nigantha Dharma,* in the Indo-Greek and Indo-Seythian periods as *Sramana Dharma;* in the Hindu period as *Jain Dharma, Syadvada Mata* or *Anekanta* Mata, in the days of Bhakti movement as *Bhavya Dharma* in the Deccan; in Rajputana as *Shravaka Dharma,* in the Punjab as the religion of the *Bhabadas* and so on.

The above small account of the antiquity, continuity and universality of Jainism is presented only to show that it has miraculously endured so long and yet preserved its identity down to the present day. Since its inception, it has ever been acting and reacting on Indian religious systems it came in contact with, and influencing, human thought and culture. It has contributed to all domains of culture, art and architecture, literature and sculpture, science and philosophy, in no mean degree. It has the noblest and the most sublime message of peace, non-violence and goodwill. It is also sublime because unlike some religions like Christianity, Islam and Buddhism, it never had any interest in religious expansion or prosetylisation. Hence, missionary ambitions and fanaticism of conversion are unknown to them. Further, Jainism is the religion which has concern not only for all human beings but also for all living beings even for the vegetable and material kingdom. It regards the entire universe filled with life. However, it is true that the most parts of its history and culture are wrapped up in obscurity and very little light has been thrown upon its great heritage.

The reason that Jainism, in spite of its sublimest message of universal love and non-violence has not expanded itself lies in its very nature. To the Jains, religion is not a world-conquering phenomenon. It simply wants to conquer one's own self—one's lust anger, greed and attachment. It is, therefore, extremely inwardly and introvert. To them religion is not object of display but interplay, it is interested in self-realization rather than expansion.

Due to this introvert nature the Jains unfortunately adopted a negativistic interpretation of their ethical virtues or vows. This was an ethical as well as a practical blunder. The later Jains even forgot the lessons of their great *Tirthankaras,* that in order to fulfil the vows, we have to cultivate both the negative and positive conditions.

Therefore, they insisted more upon the negative aspect of non-violence and limiting themselves to abstain from injury to others. Non-violence must be positive and constructive—which implies compassion, service and sympathy. Similarly this will be a spiritual error if we equate celibacy only with freedom from sexual urge and do not emphasise upon its positive side that lies in creative application of accumulational power. Unless we combine the negative and positive dimensions of celibacy, we will find mendicants and ascetics who observe celibacy to be parasitic, easily irritable and upholders of various superstitions. Positive celibacy can lead to the development of creative and aesthetic faculties.

Lets us consider few examples from the legendary history of Jainism falsifying this one-sided approach. Lord Neminath commended abstinence from meat-eating, while the positive efforts for the protection of animals from slaughter also came to be regarded as religious, when he refused to marry in order to save the animals gathered for marriage-feast. Lord Parsvanath, while even in the state of penance, raised his voice to save the snake amidst burning woods. He unambiguously declared that their penance and rites which entailed the death of innocent creatures anti-religious. Lord Mahavira did not keep the spiritual principle of equality of all souls confined to the individual life, but applied it, as a religious principle, to social welfare. He waged a crusade against caste-system based on birth. Similarly, he did not consider more abstinence from falsehood as adequate for the fulfilment of the vow of truth. He regarded silent witnessing of falsehood without protest as equivalent to the falsehood inspired by fear. So, fully conscious of the extremely revengeful and wrathful nature of Gosalaka, he did not hesitate to reveal his identity, although, if Mahavira had remained silent, none would have charged him of violating the vow of non-violence. Thus, we can see living and positive non-violence in the lives of the great Jain Tirthankaras.

The other reason why Jainism has been branded as negativistic is that its creative and positive side has not been highlighted. It has always been projected as a religion which stands for individual emancipation, penance and suffering. Few people know about the great depositories of ancient literature, the beautiful temples and art and architecture of the Jains. In these depositories of knowledge (*jnana-bhandaras*), not only the Jain scriptures have been preserved but treatises on various subjects have also been collected and preserved without any sectarian bias, like medicine, surgery, astrology, astronomy, palmistry, mythology, rhetoric and the different systems of philosophy, even of the non-Jain systems. Similarly, the colossal image of Gommatsara at Sravanbelgola and the art of Dilwara temple at Mount Abu are unmistakable proofs of the creative and aesthetic tastes of the Jainis. Few communities in India can match the Jainis in social and public welfare activities like setting up numerous educational institutions, charitable dispensaries and *dharmashalas.* Hence, what is needed is to focus upon the positive side of Jain religious history.

Another reason for a general distaste and apathy towards Jain religion is its attitude towards God. India is by and large a religion and God-intoxicated country. Whether it is art or music, religion or philosophy, all are directed to the divine. Any ideology which denies God, fails to command the respect of the people. There might be good metaphysical and moral reasons to deny God, but the common mind from the pragmatic stand point, needs a support. Very few people are interested in the subtle logical proofs for and against the existence of God and a large number of people accept God as a matter of faith. It is the yearning of the soul to posit a supreme deity. Even the Jains, although they denied a creator God, extolled their *Arhats* and the *Siddhas* to the same status of supreme divinity. They, perhaps, denied God to raise man to the status of God, as the human beings have infinite potentialities—infinite faith, knowledge power and bliss. In other words, man can be omniscient and also omnipotent. Hence, Jainism created its own Gods with the difference; whereas others are satisfied with only one god. The Jains have innumerable gods. Like the Vedic incarnations, the Tirthankaras come to the world for the good of humanity, though they are not gods. Here we find a conflict between knowledge and faith. From the point of view of knowledge and intellect, there is denial of God and godhead but faith restores them in one form or the other. However, this half-hearted approach to God makes Him listless and lusterless hence they had to develop the same ritualism as we find in the Brahminical religion. But even then God of Jainism in the form of *Arhats* is a poor substitute. He is neither a creator nor a benefactor. He does neither good nor evil. He is immune from praise or blame. He is devoid of material excellences and is incapable of bestowing any reward or punishment. The soul gets pleasure or pain according to one's *karmas.* However, *karmas* are inert and material. We require a principle which can guide and coordinate the actions. Jainism, unfortunately cannot provide such a conscious principle and it therefore degenerates into formulating an unconscious teleology like the *Sankhyas.* In Jainism, neither the self nor the *karmas* are autonomous. Self is conditioned by the *karmas* for its progress or regress. To hold that *karmas* themselves lead to results like drinking of liquour produces intoxication or milk produces health is to accept the principle of unconscious teleology. However, there is another advantage to uphold the autonomy of *karma i.e.,* to make the person absolutely responsible to his *karmas.* If God is regarded as the bestower of result of *karmas,* man's responsibility is somewhat shifted to God. In this way, Jainism becomes a religion of self-help. Man is the master of his own destiny. He does not stand for the grace of God. This is like the Gita message of lifting oneself by oneself or Buddha's message of "Be a lamp into yourself". The Gita combines effort (*Purushartha*) with fate (*daiv*) and also brings in God to avoid any moral dilemma of derailment. Buddhists have to axis, neither of the soul nor of God. With the result, its moral fabric is always in the need of metaphysics which they openly want to avoid. The Jains have, however, concentrated on 'self' and 'self-development'. They have meticulously drawn fourteen stages (*Gunasthanas*) of the spiritual development. Their aim is to transmute the *Atman* into *Parmatman* as Kundakunda, Yogindu, Pujyapada etc. have advocated. But the Atman becomes *Parmatman,* even if it falls short of the glamour and grandeur of a theistic God. The Atman in its perfect state is equipped with four-fold infinities (*ananta-chatustaya*) but even then he is neither a creator nor preserver of the world. To the Jains, the creation is eternal and beginningless. Even the conception God has to answer the question of the first cause. The Jains propound the theory of eternality of creation instead of God. Perhaps they thought that there were difficulties also in the theistic hypothesis of God as the first cause.

Another cause of opposition towards the Jains might be traced to its attitude to the authority of the Vedas. There were the *Sankhyas* and the *Mimansakas* among the orthodox systems who had frankly disowned God in their metaphysical formulations but accepted the authority of Vedas. Jains had their own scriptures called the *Agamas,* as vast and as spiritual as the Vedas. Hence they did not accept the authority of the Vedas. This was too much for the Vedic priests. Vedas were regarded as impersonal and eternal hence the most sacred. It did not belong to a sect or community. It belonged to the entire mankind. Hence to deny their authority incurred the wrath of the scholastics as well as the priests. Manu defined a heretic or nastika not one who denies God, but who does not accept the Vedas as the supreme authority (*Nastiko ved nindakah*).

Thus by denying the existence of Supreme God, Jains alienated themselves from the faith of the common people and by not accepting the authority of the Vedas, they incurred the displeasures of scholars and the priests and this further alienated them from the mainstream of Indian ethos and religious life. Besides, some customs and practices of the Jain monks in the name of religion, like not to take bath at all or wash their clothes, or practising nudity, etc. come into conflict with the accepted socio-cultural norms of society. This also might have strengthened the aversion of the people against the Jains in general. By their avowed opposition to animal sacrifice and caste system, the Jains had already annoyed the vested interests in society, namely the priests, who were the leaders of the society, who could easily mobilise the opinion of the people against the Jains.

So far the ethical teachings of the Jains are concerned, they had remarkable similarities with the Vedik ethos. For example, soul and *karma* are the cornerstones of both the Vedic and the Jain thought. The five great vows of the Jains are no different from five codes of conduct (*Panchshila*) of the Buddhist or the Five Moral Principles (*Yamas*) of the Vedic thought. The Jains, no doubt have shown deeper concern and more rigid formulations of these vows but they introduced extremism; hence they were beyond the reach of the common man. Thus, the code of conduct of the Jains remained confined to the monks and nuns only evil the lay people and the householders adopted a pragmatic style of life. This explains why Jainism could not become a religion of the common people. Today Acharya Tulsi, therefore, is taking great pains to convert Jainism as a faith of the common man (*Jan Dharma*) by bringing moderation into the five great vows called *Anuvratas,* which can be practised easily by the common people. This is like the middle path—which is neither too high nor too low.

However, Jainism is more relevant today than before. The world has been reeling under a culture of violence. It has almost reached the stage to threaten our existence. Either, we accept non-violence or face non-existence. Even our civil life has been so much-permeated with violence, that a culture of peace and non-violence is not an intellectual luxury but a sociological imperative. Violence has lost its dynamics hence we have to see how we can reconstruct our socio-cultural life on the basis of non-violence. Non-violence demands a new economics, a new politics, a new education and above all a new style of life. Non-violence today is a 'yes to life' and violence is 'no to life'. Jainism can provide intellectual basis for the practice of non-violence through its non-absolutistic metaphysics (*Anekantavada*) and relativistic epistemology (*syadvaḍa*). Ethical basis on non-violence is almost common to all religions but the extension of non-violence to thought and form of judgment is unique to Jainism. Instead of appreciating the great merit of non-absolutistic doctrine, scholars like Sankar, Ramanujan and others have levelled charges of contradiction, doubt or uncertainty. The Vedantic Acharyas forget that even they recognise the levels of reality and knowledge. Reality is multi-dimensional and therefore we can speak of it differently if we view it from different standpoints or angles. The root of most of our conflict and quarrel lies in the fact that we think ourselves as the sole possessor of truth and rest in the clutches of devil and falsehood. Jainism, in spite of rejecting any interpretation of reality, accords its place in the variegated world. Jainism did not come to destroy but to accept them all. Such a catholic and liberal outlook alone can be the basis of a world religion.

But when we examine the claims of the doctrine of the manifoldness of Truth from the metaphysical standpoint, we have some difficulties when the Jains say that each of philosophical positions of Nyaya, Vedanta or Buddhism is correct from their respective standpoints. To say so sounds confusing. The difficulty arises when we want to know which is the truth. Every system of thought takes it as true. Jains too, who claim to profess non-absolutism and relativistism, do not like to buzz even an inch from their own position of 'six substances or nine categories'. Like every system, the Jains also stick to their positions. Hence, advocacy of non-absolutism does not restrict them to hold fast to their own positions. To extol Syadvada as the impartial arbitrator could have any meaning when the Jains would not have tried so assiduously to stick to their metaphysical or ethical positions. At best, one can say that the Jain conception of reality avoids the Scylla of fluxism and the Charybdis of illusionism, when it holds origination, cessation and persistence as the fundamental characteristics of reality. But to advocate relativism on the epistemological level and absolutism in metaphysics are quite apparent in Jainism.

Like non-absolutism, there is a small contradiction in the Jain concept of non-violence. No doubt, non-violence is the greatest contribution of Jainism to the world, but it becomes almost impractical or Utopian when in their zeal to be more and more universal, they try to posit life in all living beings, vegetable kingdom and even in material world. It means that the practice of absolute non-violence is absolute non-sense or an impossibility. Our life depends upon some kind of violence. However, we can insist on practicing only progressive non-violence as a practical measure. Hence absolute vow of non-violence in only an ideal, an Utopia. This is most tragically reflected in the Jain pledge "not to harm any innocent creatures." On the face of this pledge, there is nothing unreasonable but if we look into its implications, it means that we have right to inflict injury to those creatures who are not innocent. To me, it seems to be a second or even a third grade of non-violence. As Jesus says : "Love thine enemies." Non-violence to be non-violent must be universal and unilateral. Non-violence loses its lustre if violence is permitted. Hatred brings hatred. Forgiveness is more manly than punishment. Mankind has to get out of violence only through non-violence. Non-violence in its dynamic condition means conscious suffering. It is a universal principle and its operation is not limited by a hostile environment. It has to be pursued even in face of violence raging around us. Non-violence is not simply non-killing, it is positive love. It knows no enemy; it does not differentiate between innocent or non-innocent. Lord Jesus also prayed for those who crucified him—"God forgive them for they know not what they have done."

There is another difficulty in the Jain practice of non-violence. Jain non-violence has been predominantly directed towards the individual behaviour. They have not been able to provide a social dimension to non-violence like the Christians, where we find a movement against conscription. The spirit of pacifism grew in the proportion Christianity expanded although they are also responsible for waging major wars of this century. For example, there was Christian movement of pacifism and abstinence from participation in war. It spread to the extent of national or international wars. Modern pacifism is the logical outcome of Christian pacifism. Now, we have world pacifist meeting and institutions like World Council of Religion for Peace, Federation of International Fellowships, etc. Jainism has been truly wedded to non-violence from the very beginning but they have confined their work of non-violence to the abstinence from cruelty to animals and man. They have hardly demonstrated collective or individual non-violence resistance against war. What to speak of the Jain monks, even Jain householders have never been able to raise voice against conscription, or increase in armaments like Rev. Fuji Guruji, Russell and others. In history, there have been some Jain monarchs like Chandragupt, Chetaka, Shrenika, Ajat Shatru, Kharvela, etc. but none of them renounced war. It means that their non-violence is more individual than socially dynamic.

Jainism, both in India and in the West has been very much misunderstood. The common perception is that it is too much rigoristic and negativistic even to the extent of being sadistic. Apart from too much of asceticism and extolling self-torure, self-suffering through fasting and other modes of penance, it goes even to celebrate "voluntary dying" (*Samlekhana*) as religious and spiritual phenomena. Common people cannot accept too much self-torture of the body. All acts of virtues like charity, benevolence, truth, non-violence, etc., are performed through this body. Human body is verily, the vehicle of all righteousness. Hence to regard flesh is a burden is not a positive outlook.

The Jains try to interpret such self-torture of the body as learning object—lessons in forbearance which is necessary for practising their cardinal vows of non-violence, truth, celibacy, non-possession, etc. The Vedic religion also emphasises the virtue of self-suffering and forbearance (*Tapasya* and *titiksha*). The Jains think that the spiritual aspirant should try to season his body and mind in such a manner that he might not succumb to physical discomforts that might come in the way of his spiritual realisation. Then, the extreme ascetic ideals are meant for the monks and nuns and not for the common householders. The lives of those monks and nuns serve as the height of ideals always reminding us of the direction our lives should take. Ideals are always ideals, they have to be kept before us as guiding principles. There ought to be reasonable gap between theory and practice. Regarding Samlekhana, the Jains want to differentiate it from simple suicide. This is like mercy killing. When somebody feels that his life has become a burden and there is no remedy to remove the growing suffering, he opts to die with equanimity rather than to demoralise him by weeping. It means that Jainism has not only taught an art of living but also art of dying most peacefully and courageously. *Samlekhana* is not a death due to any despondency or frustration, it is dying without attachment or aversion in perfect peace.

Jains might advance ecological basis of practising austerity and limitation of wants and limitation to consumption in view of the havoc the depletion of natural resources plays on environment. Unless we put a limit to our extravagance rooted in our materialistic hedonistic life style, we are bound to face an ecological disaster. This is the real spirit behind Jain theory of 'limits to consumption'. The Jain scripture enjoins upon us not only not to injure any living being but also not to damage the vegetation or misuse water or other natural resources. When there is water and energy crisis in the offing, Jainism seems quite relevant. Mad rush for the use of fuel-propelled car or aeroplane is showing the danger-signal as coal or oil are non-renewable sources of energy. Perhaps we might be forced to use more and more bicycle or animal-driven carts in future. Who knows, we might be compelled to use our feet and legs to cover short distances as a matter of necessity. The Jain monks do not use vehicles and we can learn from their examples. Whatever might be said in the defence of the Jains against the charge of asceticism or rigorism. There is some truth in it. If religion is not only for a few monks or highly realised souls, we have to work out a middle path between hedonism and rigorism, between extravagance and absolute abstinence or non-possession to a reasonable standard. It cannot afford to remain on the ivory-tower of extreme rigorism, it must come down to earth. Some of the Jain Acharyas have realised it and have amended the rules of conduct. A most puritan Jain Acharya Tulsi also had to create a new order of probationer monks and nuns called Samans and Samanis, who are allowed to use vehicles and planes and live even with the house-holders, observing their other religious codes of purity, celibacy and strict limitation of consumption. Muni Sushil Kumarji, Chitra Bhanuji, Bhattarak Charu Kisti, Acharya Chandana, etc. have relaxed most of the old rules of travel, residing in private houses, keeping some money, etc, which might lead to degeneration as well. A craze for publicity has seized many modern Jain Acharyas, which is repugnant to spiritual life. The spirit behind principle of penance and austerity might be good, but when they are followed and practised in letters without consideration of time and space, they serve more as obstacles than help.

Vegetarianism is practised to minimise violence in society and the world. Those who commit cruelty to the animals and birds will not deter to do the same with their fellow beings, when circumstances might arise. Non-vegetarianism is also not necessary for the preservation of human life. It creates a feeling of animal passion of torpor and insensitivity. It also increases our lust to satisfy our palates at the cost of the life of others. Besides, the existence of birds and beasts are also very relevant for the conservation of environment. From medical point of view, the disease in the body of the slaughtered animals or beasts is transmitted into our body. Economically, for a non-vegetarian person, we need at least four-five times more land than we need for vegetarian one. There might be many moral and spiritual arguments and also some counter-arguments. But if we want a non-violent society, we have also to develop a foodhabit based on non-violent style of life and non-injury to others. In the west, there has been a growing movement in favour of vegetarianism, bereft of any religious dogma and this is encouraging. The Jains like the Vaishnavas must be credited to follow vegetarianism more scrupulously and as a community, on religious considerations. This is a tragedy that meat-eating has almost become a fashion today. Even outstanding environmentalists and peace-activists do not bother about the ethics of vegetarianism. Spiritual progress does demand at some stage that we should cease to kill our fellow creatures for the satisfaction of our bodily wants. To quote Goldsmith :

No flocks that range the valley free
To slaughter I condemn
Taught by the Power that Pities me
I learn to pity them.

Animal food is also unsuited to those who would curb their passions. Even from aesthetic point of view, slaughter of animals or birds for our food is not desirable.

However, it is wrong to overestimate the importance of food in the formation of character or in subjugating the flesh. Diet is powerful factor no doubt but to sum up religion in terms of diet, as is often done in India, is wrong. It is to disregard all other restraints like exploitation, profiteering, hoarding, etc. ahimsa is not a mere matter of dialectics, it transcends it. What a man eats or drinks matters little; it is the self-denial that matters. A man, always unscrupulous in his food habit is an utter stranger to ahimsa and a pitiful wretch if he is a slave to selfishness and passions and is hard of heart.

Jainism, being rooted in the Sraman and wandering-ascetic tradition lays great stress upon *tapasya* on suffering for the purification of soul. It includes suffering to body, study of scriptures, meditation, etc. There are quite a number of Jain monks and nuns as well as householders who go on fast for very long periods like one month or more. There are Jain monks who walk over almost fire-like heated sands or walking bare footed in the winter and so on. It means there is more emphasis upon external *tapasya* in Jainism. Even Lord Mahavira is called as long-sufferer (*dirgha tapasvi*). But it is a matter of consideration to know, how far the external *tapasya* have influenced the internal and spiritual life. This seems that integral view of *tapasya* as taught by Lord Mahavira having both the external as well as the internal dimension of *tapasya* has been ignored by the Jain tradition. The internal tapasya consists of deep study, meditation and purification of mind and soul. To think that fasting alone is the remedy for purification of soul is a lopesided thinking. The real test should be reducing oneself to the zero, practising natural humility. In fact, non-imposition of oneself is the test of non-possession. There is a great fascination for swelling number of monks and nuns in every order. One's religious empire is known by the number of monks and nuns he has. The real dynamism in Jainism will, in fact, come through concentration on education and practising of moral, ethical and spiritual life. By simply swelling the number of monks and nuns through initiation, we hardly add vigour to Jainism. Spirituality consists inner development and unfolding of man. There should be freedom for a monk or nun to go back to the life of a householder freely and without any compunction or disregard in society. To lead an ascetic life with compulsion is not only atrocious and counter-productive but also unspiritual. Similarly, instead of taking the life-long great vows in the beginning through ritual of initiation, one should be allowed to proceed through stages. To initiate a boy or girl of young age into the order of a recluse or monk or nun and not allow him or her to go back to householder's life is akin to committing violence. Such unwilling persons only add to the burden of the order and spread many evils. Unlike Jainism, the Hindu society is more accommodative to the monks or nuns who wish to return to the householders life. Except a few, Jain ascetic order hardly presents a picture of first grade original thinkers like Swami Vivekananda, Ramakrishna, Dayanand, Raman Maharsi, because they are overburdened with external asceticism and ritualism.

Like all other religions and culture, Jainism too has two dimensions—external and internal. In its external aspects, includes rites and rituals, art and architecture, temples and monasteries, forms of worship and festivals, food-habits modes of behaviour, etc. But the heart and soul of Jainism is the spirit of world-negation, because it aims at breaking the chain of birth and rebirth and enable to attain salvation. Hence, it relies mainly on the purification of mind and heart, which is the path of liberation. Such a world-view of religion is bound to be individualistic and based on self-realisation. For such a life, what is needed is self-study, introspection, meditation, suffering and a life of detachment. But the difficulty is that such a hard and rigoristic life cannot become universal. Its emphasis lay upon cessation and control of desires. The sole concern is self-realisation and any obstacle coming through our desires must be overcome. This attitude of controlling our desires is reflected even in Brahminical religion and, therefore, there has been sufficient interaction between them and also some amount of synthesis. But Jainism has been more attuned towards denial of the worldly life of pleasure and comforts. However, in its zeal to curb our desires and lust, Jainism has lost social interest to some extent. It has created a world of its own in isolation fortified by puritanism and rigorism. Activity in world is not unwarranted, what is unwarranted is our attachment to it. Jainism unfortunately, in order to give emphasis upon detachment, has adopted a life-negating attitude to the world. Hence, it has become a religion of toils and tears, fasts and sufferings, rather than of joy and bliss.

REFERENCES

1. *Sacred Books of the East,* Vols. XXII & XLV (introduction).
2. *Satyartha Darpana,* p. 97 quoted by J.P. Jain in *Jainism : The*

Oldest Living Religions, Jain Cultural Research Society, Benaras, 1951, p. 41.

3. Presidential Address, C.A.S., 1898.
4. *Rgveda,* X.12.166; VIII. 8-24; *Yajurveda,* IX.251; XXV.19.; *Samveda, Id.* 103.
5. *Bhagavata Purana,* II.7.9.10.
6. Jain Antiquary, Arrah, XV. Vol. II. P. 58 (Article by Prof. S. Srikanta Shastri).
7. S.N. Gokhale, *Indian Theosophist.*
8. G. Satyanarayan Murti, *Jain Gazette,* 1916, p. 73.

4

Jain Theory of Non-Absolutism and the Law of Contradiction

The most formidable attack on the Jain theory of non-absolutism has been from the side of Law of Contradiction, as reflected in the treatises of Vedantic and Buddhist Acharyas. While the Law of Identity says that A is A, the Law of Contradiction holds that A is not B. These are simple statements of truth. Hence, when Syadvada ascribes two contradictory predications, *asti* and *nasti,* to the same subject, there is bound to arise a frame of inconsistency. This is true to the commonsense as well as to the demands of logic. But if we remember that no statement can be properly and correctly understood without reference to the context or perspective, there will be no difficulty. There is logic of life which is necessary for the proper understanding of context. Jainism respects the laws of logic, but it is not also oblivious to the actualities.

In Brahma Sutra,[1] there is a passage charging the Jainas of violating the Law of Contradiction while discussing the principle of non-absolutism. Apparently the charge seems to be true on the ground of the impossibility of the presence of contradictory qualities in one and the same substance contained in the theory of seven paralogisms. The Law of Contradiction means that two contradictory terms B and not B cannot both be true and false at the same time of one and the same thing 'A'. In other words, two contradictory propositions cannot be both *true.* One must be false. For example, a man cannot be both *alive* and *dead.* This means that the products of thought should be free from inconsistency and contradiction to be valid in Hamiltonian sense.[2] Mill also says in other words that in order to be true, a thing must agree with the reality of things.[3] Pragmatists always emphasise upon the 'context' which is neglected by the Formal Logic.[4] Even mathematical logicians admit the conception of universe of discourse in the sense of "a given context, or range of significance."[5]

To the Advaita Vedanta, Being and Non-being are *contraries,* not *contradictories.* Reality is Being, Non-being is unreal; but there is the third order of reality which is neither Being nor Non-being. This is called *Maya.* Let us illustrate it from the point of view of the Upanishadic account of the self, which is described as *mobile* and yet *immobile, distant* and yet *imminent.*[6] One can ask, how the Upanishads could afford to violate the Law of Contradiction so flagrantly. Sankar says that there is no fallacy here because two contradictory statements have been made from two separate standpoints. Self is said to be *mobile* when it is associated with the powers of the limiting adjunct, of being an internal organ[7], but it is called *immobile* when viewed from ultimate point of view. Similar such contradictory predications are found at other places in the Upanishads or elsewhere but Sankar has no alternative but to reconcile them with the help of his multi-valued logic, which is nothing different from affirmative-negative predictions (*asti-nastivada*). Here I do not find any radical difference in the methodology adopted by Sankar and the Jains. Both employ and adhere to the Principle of Standpoints. Sankar adopts three standpoints, while the Jains adopt seven-fold standpoints. One may or may not accept the Jain theory of identity-indifference or six-fold substances of soul or not soul, but its epistemological approach is not only practical but also logical. Like Sankar, Ramanujan seems to be equally prejudiced against the Jain theory when he asks : How can we say that the same thing *is* and *is not* at the same time?[8] However, Ramanujan forgets that if we describe a thing both from the standpoint of underlying substance (*Dravya*) and its modifications (*Paryaya*), we can predicate both *'is'* and *'is not'* at the same time. Even Ramanujan's metaphysics is the doctrine of *one* and *many*, when we talk about the multiple *jivas* and the multi-verse. Hence, Ramanujan's theory of identity—in-difference becomes itself a sufficient argument in favour of Jain theory of Syadvada. If Ramanujan can find both conscious (*chit*) and unconscious (*achit*) in his one Brahman, how can he find fault with the very logical calculus of *asti-nasti* in Jaina doctrine of relativity of judgments. He cannot rise above from the same ladder which he prefers to destroy. Logic is to systematise and rationalise what experience offers. Even Vedanta ultimately relies on experience to prove the triple nature of reality as existence, consciousness and bliss—*sat, chit* and *ananda*.

Vijnabhiksu attacks from a different angle when he says that two fundamentally opposite things cannot be reconciled into one object, unless the qualitative differences are recognised as true. But if the differences are recognised as true, it amounts to the vedantic position. How can ultimate *differences* be reconciled with the ultimate *identity* of Brahman. Either they should accept *identity* as ultimate or differences as ultimate but not *both*. However, the Jains can avoid such a difficulty by accepting the differences from relative standpoints. We can speak of *existence* and *non-existence* of the same thing from two standpoints without being inconsistent. Both existence and non-existence co-existing in the same thing is called contradictory because both of them are taken as whole characteristics. But they can be easily reconciled if we take them as past-characteristics. Even Vallabhacharya labours under the same misconception[9] when he insists upon the fact that differences can be reconciled only in the Absolute Brahman, who assumes the form of the Jivas for the enjoyment of bliss. However, it is difficult to follow how the formless Brahman assumes different forms or how the *one* becomes, *many?* If the law of contradiction is not violated here, the position of the Jains is also safe when contradictory attributes are said to inhere in the same object from the different relative standpoints. While accepting the possibility of reconciliation of the contradictory attributes in the same object from the different standpoints, Sri Kantha[10] outright denies that the Jains ever adhere to the relativistic logic. Nimbaraka,[11] who himself, is an able exponent of the principle of identity difference with regard to the nature of reality, also refuses to admit the application of this very principle in matters of relativistic logic. His commentator Sri Nivasacharya says that the justification for admitting the principle of identity-in-difference lies in the *Sruti* and not in logic.[12] According to Bhaskara, if non-absolutism is universal (*Anekanta*) it becomes absolute (*ekanta*), if not, it is nothing definite. Thus "tossed between the two horns of the dilemma non-absolutism evaporates".[13] However, Bhaskara fails to find distinction made by the Jains between the valid-non-absolutism (*samyak-anekanta*) and invalid-non-absolute (*mithya-anekanta*).[14] To be valid *anekanta* must not be absolute but relative. But the unconditionality of Anekanta or Syadvada is quite different from the normal meaning of unconditionality. For example, when I say, "I do not know myself," there is no contradiction between knowledge and ignorance. Similarly, in the sentence, "I am undecided", there is at least one decision that I am undecided about. These critics fail to understand that contradictory characteristics of reality are interpreted as co-existent in the same object from different points of view without any offence to logic.

Even Buddhist logicians like Dharmakirti,[15] Pragnakara Gupta[16] and Archat[17] redicule the contradictory predications of the *asti-nasti* of the Jains, least realising the fact of standpoints. They object that it cannot be both eternal as well as non-eternal. They fail to understand that even Lord Buddha refuted both eternalism as well as fluxism and propounded the doctrine of dependent origination. In fact, he accepts the position of non-absolutism. Buddhist Acharyas unnecessarily try to raise an issue that the same substance cannot have two forms or dimensions, when they know that the Jain's predications of these contradictory attributes are made from two standpoints—*Sva-paksha* and *Parapaksha.* Hence, there is no violation of the law of contradiction.

Almost all Buddhist Acharyas, like the Vedantic Acharyas, charge Jain theory of Anekantvada or Syadvada of violating the law of contradiction in different ways. The same refrain of Dharmakiriti is repeated by Pragnakara, Archat, Santarakshita,[18] Karnakgomi,[19] and others,[20] in different ways and with different sets of examples. Jayarasibhatia's *Tattopalva Simha* is a book of critique par-excellence. It does not want to establish the existence of any reality. According to Jayarasi Bhatt, reality is neither eternal nor non-eternal, nor both nor even neither. This means that we cannot have one sided affirmation and this is the spirit behind Syadvada. Jayaras[21] might hurl any uncharitable abuse upon the Jains (as Digambaras) but he himself accepts the position of the Jains in establishing his own theory. Acharya Vyomsiva[22] scores a novel point when he says that the law of non-absolutism, if applied to the concept of Mukti will result in a queer situation as where a liberated person will be liberated from one standpoint and a worldly person from different standpoint and consequently if non-absolutism is applied to non-absolutism, it will involve the fallacy of *infinite regress.* We can easily meet such objections. For example, any soul which has been in bondage from the beginningless time becomes free from the shackles of *karma,* hence it is both free from the point view of present time and *not-free* from the point of view of past.

The non-absolutistic standpoint is the typical standpoint of identity-in-difference whose germs are also found in the Vedas,[23] the Upanishads,[24] and Buddha's backing.[25] Even in Brahma Sutra, Acharya Asamrathya and Auddolome[26] were upholdres of this theory of identity-in-difference. Many Vedantis like Bhaskaracharya and Nimbarka uphold this theory of identity-in-difference. Sankhya accepts the theory or real transformation, which means that it accepts the reality as *eternal as well as* having changing forms. Yoga also accepts the theory of real transformation. Kumarila also accepts the dual nature of soul.[27]

Hence, Hemchandra says that the Buddhists have no right to refute Anekanta as they regard the same knowledge with different dimensions; Nayayikas and Vaisesikas also cannot object to it since they accept different pictures of the same reality; so also the Sankhyas too cannot criticise non-absolutism as the same Prakriti contains threefold attributes. Hence, non-absolutism is accepted in spirit by almost all the traditions of India.

However, we cannot deny that Vedantic acceptance of difference is only on formal level. They are not real. Brahma is unchangeable and immutable. In Sankhya, transformation or change is only relevant to the level of attributes, it does not affect the Prakriti, which is eternal and real. Even Kumarila,[28] who accepts the theory of difference, keeps its substance intact and without any change. Whether we accept Jain metaphysics or not, we should have no objection in accepting the epistemological calculus of multi-dimensionality, because it is based on experience and realism. The limitation and conditional character of the judgment and the possibility of equally valid alternative judgments from other points of view are clearly acknowledged. This does not mean that the Jain philosophers deny the mind and its active contributions. He treats the mind as an instrument of discovery and not a creator of facts. The function of logic is to rationalise and systematise what experience offers. A real is only a part of a system woven together by a network of relations and attributes from which it cannot be divorced. The logic of Einstein's special theory of relativity is also very similar to Syadvada. There is no absolute significance to the length, mass, or energy of a rod or to the time interval between two events in Einstein's theory—they acquire a physically measurable value relative to particular system or frames of references. Different values of these attributes in different frames in relative motion are, however, related to one another. I do not say that the ancient Jains had anticipated all these sophisticated issues of modern science. Einstein and Neils Bohr were presumably unaware of Syadvada, yet they arrived at something strikingly similar to it from entirely different considerations. This is presumably because the logical issues involved in synthesising apparently contradictory but equally valid observations into a holistic view were really the same.

REFERENCES

1. Brahma Sutra, II.2.23.
2. Hamilton, *Lectures,* Vol. III, pp. 25-26.
3. J.S. Mill, *Examination of Hamilton's Philosophy,* 4th ed. pp. 564-470.
4. F.C.S. Schiller, *Logic For Use,* Ch. on Formal Theories of Judgement.
5. L.S. Stebbing, *An Introduction to Logic,* p. 55.
6. *Isa Upanishad,* Verse 5.
7. *Isa Upanishad,* Verse 4.
8. Brahma-sutra (*Sri Bhasya),* II.2.23.
9. Vallabhacharya, *Brahma Sutra* (*Anu Bhasya),* II. 2.33.
10. Sri Kantha, *Brahma Sutra* (*Sri Kantha Bhasya),* II.2.33
11. Nimbaraka, *Brahma Sutra* (*Nimbarka Bhasya),* II.2.33
12. Brahma Sutra (*Bhaskara Bhasya),* II.2.33.
13. S. Mookerjee, *The Jain Philosophy of Non-Absolutism,* Calcutta, 1944, p. 78.
14. Samanta Bhadra, *Apta-Mimamsa,* Karika-108.
15. *Pramana Varttika,* III.108-184.
16. *Praman Varttikalankara,* p. 142.
17. *Hetu-bindu* (*Tika),* p. 146.
18. *Pramana Varttika Sva Vritti Tika,* p. 109.
19. *Vigyapti Matrata Siddhi,* II.2.
20. *Tattvopalava Simha,* pp. 78-79.
21. Vyom Biva Tika on *Prasastapada Bhasya,* p. 365.
22. Rg Veda, II.3.23. *Ekam sad Vipra bahuda badanti.*
23. *Isa,* 5,4.
24. *Digha Nikaya,* Pottpada Sutta.
25. *Brahma Sutra,* 1.4. 20-21.
26. *Yogasutra* (Vyasa Bhasya), 1.4.33.
27. Kumarila, *Mimamsa Sloka-Varttika,* 28. (Ahuavada).

5

Relevance of Anekant in Modern Times

Modern times are marked by an era of crisis in the realm of human civilisation. The reason is that we give so much attention to short-term and local problems that long-term and global problems continue to be neglected. Secondly, life has become more intricately interdependent and complex. So simpler solutions no longer suffice. A world civilisation is fast emerging and we cannot afford to solve our problems with a parochial temper and sectarian outlook. For human survival, we need human cooperation on a plenatary scale able to deal with rapidly increasing complexities. The critical problems are so complex that we need a philosophy equally complex to grapple with them. One dimensional man in a multi-dimensional world-crisis will be out of joint. Inter-existence is the positive option for mankind. Either there is organic growth of mankind or there is organic destruction of human civilisation. Not only is it too late in history to convert all of mankind to Christianity, or Islam or Jainism (or to communism, or capitalism or any other ism), but also to some metaphysical principles which we have been cherishing since antiquity. The growth of scientific knowledge and outlook has destroyed most of our false dogmas and superstitions but it has failed to provide us knowledge that could sublimate our animal and selfish nature. Animality has been dominating our individual as well as social behaviour. Hence, our life has become full of tensions, turmoils and disorders. Therefore, although we are outwardly pleading for world-peace and non-violence, yet we have been preparing for war. This is the crisis of modern times that we aspire for peace but prepare for the formidable funeral procession of mankind.

Humanity is tottering today upon the brink of self-annihilation for lack of understanding, which includes understanding ourselves and understanding each other. It is a time of tragic importance for the world because even before the shadows cast by one war are lifted fully, the skies yet again become overcast with dark threatening clouds. Hence, at no period of human history man was in need of sound philosophy than today. As war begins in the minds of men, it is in the minds of men that the defence of peace should be built. Today, if a person does not agree with me, he is wicked, if a country does not agree with my country, it is wicked as if there is no half-way, no neutrality. So ultimately it is our warring ideologies that are at the root of world-tension. But ideologies or philosophies depend upon our way of philosophising. Hence Locke rightly felt that epistemological problems are prior to all others. An epistemological reorientation will influence metaphysical grounding which in turn will determine our socio-ethico-political views. Any solution can ultimately be achieved through knowledge free from confusion and prejudices.

Since things have many characters, they are the objects of all sided knowledge. The knowledge which determines the full meaning of an object through the employment of one-sided knowledge is partial knowledge. Hence we should discard all forms of absolute judgments, otherwise truth would be violated. Reality has got innumerable characteristics. A valid knowledge is defined as that which gives us knowledge of a thing in its various aspects. All expressions are somehow real. All objects have got innumerable characters, hence all things are multidimensional or Anekantic.

The world is the store-house of great chaos in thought. All the confusion of thought which is prevailing in the world is the outcome of inexhaustive research and acceptance of a part for the whole. Almost all our disputes only betray the pigheadedness of the blind men who spoke differently about an elephant. The outstanding personalities like Sri Aurobindo, Raman Maharshi, etc, spoke to us in a world overorganised by ideological fanaticism, that truth is not exclusive or sectarian. Every idol however noble it may seem is ultimately a Moloch that devours its worshippers. It is fatal to treat the relative and the home-made as though it were the absolute. It is only intellectual clarity which will resolve all conflict and rivalry. All dogmatism owes its genesis to the partiality of outlook and fondness for a line of thinking to which a person has accustomed himself. This is imperialism and aggressiveness in thought. When the one party or another thinks himself the sole possessor of absolute truth, it becomes natural that he should think of his neighbours absolutely in the clutches of Error or the Devil. Today, one man or one country fight with the other because their views vary. Views are bound to vary because we are guided by different conditions, thought and attitudes. Hence, it is wrong to think oneself right and the rest others wrong. Here Syadvada-Anekantvada represents the highest form of Catholicism coupled wonderfully with extreme conservatism, a most genuine and yet highly dignified compromise better than we can ever imagine.

We must realise that there is other's view point as our own. This can happen when one puts oneself into another's shoes or gets under the skin of others. This is called sympathy which is the act of reproducing in our minds the feelings of another. Gandhiji once told : "I advise a man not from my standpoint but from his. I try to put myself in his shoes. When I cannot do so. I refuse to advise." He once said : " I am myself a Puritan but for others a Catholic".

Syadvad or Anekantavada is adoption of the safe and secure middle path leaving the two extremes. It means that virtue has many facets. There is a place for the penance of a saint, chastity of a woman, innocence of a child, bravery of a hero, etc. As a lover of nature, one can equally enjoy the rain during rainy season, coolness of winter and heat of summer. Similarly, life is not a straight road. There are too may complexities in it. It is not like a train which once started keeps running. The real is a variable constant. It is being and non-being, unity and plurality, the universal and the particular rolled into one. A thing is neither an absolute unity nor split into an irreconcilable plurality. It is both unity and plurality all the time. There is no opposition between unity of being and plurality of aspects. Similarly, things are neither exclusively particular, nor are they exclusively universal, but they are a concrete realisation of both. The two elements can be distinguished by reflective thought, but cannot be rent asunder. A real is neither a particular nor universal in an exclusive manner, but a synthesis which is different from both severally and jointly though embracing them in its fold. A real is *sui generis.*

Although Syadvada-Anekantavada is not a complete logic, it does involve a basic principle that seems to be essential to the kind of philosophy needed to account for, and to deal with, the complexities of our emerging world civilisation. The two-valued logic developed presupposes the principle of excluded middle as most basic—X is either A or non-A but not both (because A and non-A are contradictions. The dynamic, dialectical, organic unities inherent in the increasingly intricate inter-dependent organisations constituting our emerging world require a more dynamic, dialectical organic logic than is presently available. Despite the fact that the two-valued logic has immense practical values when used judiciously, it is still not adequate to account for all of the vital developments in human society.

It is so difficult to say objectively anything fundamental about today's civilisation or modern man because "all of us are caught in the same prejudices". Only a man who is "wholly of the present" can say something important about the present-day world, and only he who has the "most intensive and extensive consciousness" of himself and his situation can hope to be such a man. What is required is "essential thinking" (Heidegger) or "total seeing" (J. Krishnamurti) by competent persons for apprehending the problems and predicaments of contemporary civilisation and giving an inkling of their possible solutions. Karl Jaspers also talks of "luminous encompassive thinking", through which contemporary political consciousness must be transformed and a new kind of politics adequate to the threat of atomic doom should be created. Dr. S. Radhakrishnan while speaking on the future of civilisation (*Kalki, the Future of Civilization,* 1929) held that to avert periodic crises of civilisation, what is required is religious idealism and "cooperation and not identification, accommodation to fellowmen and not imitation of them, and toleration and not absolutism". Thus if we want to save our civilization from atomic annihilation, we have to encourage Anekant culture. However, Anekant philosophy of life should not be confused with contradictionism, indeterminism, scepticism or *solipsism.* When we look to the particular merits of each side, there is no contradiction. Application of existence and non-existence to the same thing is contradiction but when existence and non-existence are asserted from different standpoints, it is not contradiction. Even in the Upanishads, we have the glimpses of how the reality reveals itself in different ways at different stages of knowledge. Hence Anekant attitude should not be equated with subjective relativism of the Sophists. It is "objective relativism" or "relative absolutism" like Whithead Bodin. However, there is no similarity with Einstein's theory of relativity. To some extent, we may find a parallel in old Pyrrohoneanism in the west. But while Pyrrohoneanism relapses into agnosticism or scepticism, there is no room for scepticism whatsoever in Jaina theory of Syadvada or Anekantvada. Scepticism means in the minimum, absence of assertion, whereas Syadvadins always *assert,* though what they assert are alternatives. Disjunctive judgment is still judgment. Each disjuction is alternatively valid. Either there is no self-complete reality or any such reality is wholly infinite, a mere demand that refuses to be actualised. The only scepticism is concerning the so-called self-complete reality. So whereas a sceptic is sceptical about any character of reality, Syadvad is quite definitely assertive. Yet he is more sceptical than any sceptic in the world so far as the definiteness of the ultimate reality is concerned. He would go beyond *avaktavya* or *shunya* so far the Advaitins and Shunyavadins are concerned with regard to their statements about the ultimate reality.

Hence, Anekant stands against all mental absolutism. We can substantiate this relativistic standpoint on the cosmo-micro-physical ground supported by Einsteinian doctrine of relativity and Maxwell's equation of electro-magnetism which go fundamentally against the notion of absolute truth. When we say, we know this, we are saying more than is strictly correct, because all we know is what happens when the waves reach our bodies. Research in psychology of thinking, perception of self and conception of self in child Psychology and psycho-analytical studies in Freudian narcissism or Adlerian power factor support relativism. From socio-cultural standpoint, the doctrine of relativism is justified for no smooth functioning of society is possible without mutual accommodation and adjustment which presupposes catholicism in thought, and sense of tolerance. In ethics and morality, we know so far relativism is dominating. In the field to logic, the doctrine of the Universe of Discourse is sometimes limited to a small portion of actual universe of things and is sometimes co-extensive with that universe. The Universe of Discourse controls the interpretation of every word. Logic of Relatives too recognises the truth of Syadvada-Anekantvad when it discusses all relations embodied in propositions.

Much of the confusion either of Buddhism or Advaita Vedanta is due to false exaggeration of the relative principles of *becoming* and *being* into absolute truths. Some is the fault with Parmenidian *Being* and Heraclitan Flux. These may be called the variety of philosophical doctrines.

Hence Anekant doctrine is the exposition of the principle of 'comprehensive perspectivism.[1]' No perspective is final or absolute unless it is understood in terms of relativity. Therefore, even Anekant (non-absolutism) is subject to Anekant (non-absolutism). If non-absolutism is absolute, it is not universal since there is one real which is absolute. And if it is not a non-absolute, it is not an absolute and universal fact. Tossed between the two horns of the dilemma, non-absolutism thus simply evaporates. But we can meet this difficulty by making a distinction between the *theory* and *practice* of *anekanta*. Every proposition of the dialectical sevenfold judgement is either complete or incomplete. In the former, we use only one word that describes one characteristic of that object and hold the remaining characters to be identical with it. On the other hand, in the incomplete judgement, we speak of truths as relative to our standpoint. In short, the complete judgment is the object of valid knowledge (*Pramana*) and the incomplete judgment is the object of aspectal knowledge (*Naya*). Hence the non-absolute consists of the absolute as its elements and as such would not be possible if there were no absolutes.

Here we can solve this difficulty by analysing the nature of unconditionality of the statement "All statements are conditional," which is quite different from the normal meaning of unconditionality. This is like the idea contained in the passage—"I do not know myself", where there is no contradiction between "knowledge" and "ignorance". In the sentence, "I am undecided", there is at least one decision that I am undecided about. Similarly, the categoricality behind a disjunctive judgment (A man is either good or bad), is not like the categoricality of an ordinary categorical judgment like "The horse is red". True the basis is always categorical but this categoricality does never clash with the proposition of being disjunctive. When a logical positivist says that "there is no metaphysics" philosophy enters through the back-door. In short, the unconditionality in the statement "All statements are conditional" is quite different from the normal conditionality. There are primarily two sources to understand the world-senses and *reason,* closely connected with two grades of reality *existence* and *essence* (Existentialism) or *existence* and *reality* (Hegel). Existence is actuality or actual verification, which is unconditional, absolute and categorical. There is no alternation or condition. But on the level of *thought* or *reason* or *essence,* there may be alternatives. But we cannot live in the world of thought alone and forget *existence.* We must also have something other than thought or reason which is unreason or irrationality. Behind reason, there is always the *unreason,* which we can give the name of *faith* (as suggested by Kant, Herder, Jacobi, etc). There are many grounds of faith—one being the scripture, which differs from one another. Jains must stick to their position. Here is definiteness. However, we cannot expect such definiteness with reason because it only offers alternative pictures—Jain, Advaita, Vaisesikas. All are equally possible. In order to avoid indefiniteness we stick to one such possibility which is chosen for us by the community we belong to, or by some superior in tuition. Thus, there comes unconditionality. However, another may choose another possibility as existence if he belongs to another community or if his genius moves into another direction. So there appears to be again alternation among existence. But this alternation is not only at the thought level. We compare thought with other thoughts. And what is comparision.[7] Comparison involves thinking and reasoning, so it is thought-process. Some are bound to admit alternation. My standpoint is only a possible one. But I cannot always fly in the air of possibilities, I must have moorings in some actuality. I must adopt one standpoint.

Jainism is against all kinds of imperialism in thought. For each community there is a special absolute. But the absolute themselves are alternatives so far as they are probables. But this is only on thought level. But when I have chosen one it is more than possible, it is existence or actual. So there is wonderful reconciliation between conditionality and unconditionality. Everything is conditional on thought level, but on the level of existence. Thus there is no real contradiction.

To avoid the fallacy of infinite regress, the Jains distinguish between valid non-absolutism (*Samyaka Anekanta*) and invalid non-absolutism (*Mithya Anekanta*). Like an invalid absolute judgment, an invalid non-absolute judgement, too, is invalid. To be valid, Anekanta must not be absolute but relative.

If we consider the above points, we cannot say that the

"theory of relativity cannot be logically sustained without the hypothesis of an absolute". Thought is not mere distinction but also relation. Everything is possible only in relation to and as distinct from others and the Law of Identity. Under these circumstances, it is not legitimate to hold that the hypothesis of an absolute cannot be sustained without the hypothesis of a relative. Absolute to be absolute presupposes a relative somewhere and in some forms, even the relative of its non-existence.

Jain logic of Anekanta is based not on abstract intellectualism but on experience and realism leading to a non-absolutistic attitude of mind. Multiplicity and unity, definability and non, definability, etc., which apparently seem to be contradictory characteristics of reality are interpreted to co-exist in the same object from different points of view without any offence to logic. They seem to be contradictory to each other simply because one of them is mistaken to be the whole truth. In fact, integrity of truth consists in this very variety of its aspects, within the rational unity of an all comprehensive and ramifying principle. The charge of contradiction against the co-presence of being and non-being in the real is a figment of a priori logic.

6

Jainism as a World Religion

The Earth Summit held at Rio held in (September 1992) and holding of this Parliament of the World's Religion the next year (August 28 to 4th September, 1993) signify that the days of national chuvinism and religious fundamentalism are numbered. We have not only to think globally but also act in a global spirit, not for any altruistic motive but for the sake of our very existence. Threat of a thermo-nuclear war has not been over, though somewhat receeded. On the other hand, terrorism has assumed the form of an undeclared world war against humanity, perhaps more heinous and more cowardly. Religious fundamentalism has proved to be the greatest danger for human rights and creativity of man. Population explosion, especially in the Third World countries and the rape of the earth under the leadership of the developed nations, necessitated by a consumerist life style, have posed an unprecedented ecological disaster.

Today, what is needed is not only a Parliament of Religions but a Parliament of the Man. Religion is for man, not man for religion. If religions fail to bind us together and liberate mankind from sectarianism and superistition, hatred and violence, it is better to be irreligious and heretic.

When we talk of religion today, it is 9/10th of rites and rituals, sacraments and ceremonies, Churches and evangical missions and only 1/10th of universal ethics and spirituality. In fact religion should be the inner nature of man that should reach a certain stage of development and unfolding plus the law of the growth of the higher evolution. Religion should be the spirit of man and not his fetters. It is a blashphemy to regard Jesus, Buddha, Mohammad etc. to be the exclusive copy right patents of the Christians, Buddhist or the Muslims respectively. What is the harm if the people of the whole world call themselves as Christians, if Christanity stands for crucification and purification of the spirit? But when Christianity is equated with Churchanity, we have a bloody Bosnia or the Middle East and then we need such an exercise of inter-faith dialogue or a Ministry of Reconciliation under the Vatican or a Parliament of World's Religions at Chicago. Religious separatism is as bad as Facism or Nazism. Personal religion is like tribalism, if not more. Hence, either we have a "Universal Religion" or no religion. If God cannot be Hindu, Muslim or Christian, how His own children become different? If the human soul has no creed, caste, colour, race or sex, why should we have creed, caste, colour, race or sex, why should we indulge in the rival bigotteries, fanatic cries, and bitter hostilites? There is only one *Religion,* though *religions* are many. Religion is, no doubt, necessary to man but no particular church or sacrament is indispensable. There are two alternatives open to us-either we *reject all religions* or *accept all religions.* But both are impracticable. Hence, the only alternative is to inculcate in ourselves a spirit of Universal Religion or Religion of Man.

To think that my religion alone is right and the rest are in the clutches of the devil, is not only imperialism of thought and fanaticism but it is also the source of hatred, animosity and violence. It is quite possible that there is truth in each of these religions. There might be different dimensions. Hence, the best way to avoid confrontation is to accept that the truth is manifold. Reality is complex and our knowledge is limited. Hence, it is safe to subscribe to the non-absolutistic frame of mind. Only such a non-violence. Compassion is the moral basis of non-violence. Unity and existence of soul is its metaphysical basis but the Doctrine of Manifoldness of Truth and non-absolutism is the unfailing ideological foundation of non-violence. All dogmatism and fanaticism owe its genesis to this partiality of outlook and fondness for a particular line of thinking. The conflict becomes not only inevitable but also irreconcilable when the advocate of a particular religion develops a fanatic zeal and refuses to view it from other angels of vision. The Jainas, in accordance with their philosophy of life, refuse to take an exclusivistic standpoint and thus tries to overcome ideological and religious conflict. This catholicism of outlook is the natural outcome and extension of non-absolutistic attitude may be regarded as a very strong foundation of a world religion. There is no quarrel and conflict with the assertions and truth-claims of the other, we have to appreciate their unique visions and assign their proper value in an impartial estimation, in the light of its inter-connection with the entire reality.

As a corrolary to this principle of non-absolutism in thought, we need a synthetic principle in life. It cannot be anything other than non-violence and peace. This is also the demand of our survival. This doctrine of non-violence seems to have arisen out of a strong sence of the unity of the universe. At the same time, there is a firm desire to escape from the material world, an attitude which would be negated by harm done to a fellow creature. This is **'reverence for life'**. It follows that equal regard be paid to the welfare of every single man, woman and child, and equal, effective and maximum opportunities of self-realisation be placed within each of all. In international affairs, the only alternative to non-inviolence is non-existence. In the social context, war, armament and Machiavellian diplomacy are not isolable phenomena. If disputes are settled on the plane of force, it is because our social life has been moving on the corresponding planes of hatred, frustration and exploitation. Non-violence to be practical must aim at a wholesale transformation in the internal government of state as well as their mutual contacts to a revision of social and economic arrangements. All institutional reorganisations require a virtue, a morality in harmony with it. Even science that violates the rhythm of nature are **satanic**. It needs universal human values like love, truth, non-violence compassion etc.

The denial of non-violence **(ahimsa)** and violation of the rhythm of nature are equivalent to violation of truth. Society that seeks truth and is governed by the principle of **Ahimsa** to enable men to comprehend reality is its greatest richness. We must understand the power as well as limits of science. Science will suffer greviously and in the end reduce itself to a mockery if all its powers are not yoked to alleviate human suffering. But unless we learn to overcome and liquidate violence, the future is dark for all. On certain occasions, violence indeed appears useful. One can solve a problem quickly with force. But violence has a tendency to lead to counter-violence and counter-violence never ends. In the case of cold war the principle of nuclear deterrence had helped promote stability, it did not create genuine peace. The last four and half decades in Europe have been merely the absence of war, which has not been real peace but a fascimile founded on fear. Non-violence is not negative but positive. It is not only absence of war or bloodshed. It points to a wholesale transformation in the socio-economic structure as well as in their psyche. It is not something an abstraction or an ideal. It is a necessity. It is the very law of our life. It is the positive Cosmic Love. It arises from development of the mental attitude in which hatred is replaced by love. We cannot create so much as one particle of dust, therefore, what right have we to destroy the very least form? True non-resistance is the one true resistance to evil. Good is all that serves life, evil is all that stifles. Good is reverence for life, evil is reverence for death. It narrows it down and cuts it into pieces. Hence, the best ethics consists is reverence for life. There is one religion—the religion of love. There is one message, the message of non-violence or Ahimsa, the message of holding one's own self in all beings. Militarism is not only anti-civilization, it is also very expensive. Pursing peace through military power places a tremendously wasteful burden on society. Hence, total disarmament is the only way out both for human survival and welfare.

Non-violence is not limited to the stoppage of war and bloodshed, it must also stop the arrogance of man towards nature. The materialistic civilization has provided a life of luxury, consumerism and extravagance. We are faced with the cruel exploitation of natural resources meant for the coming generations. Hence, our luxurious life is at the cost of the rape of the earth. Hence either we adopt a life of plain living and high thinking or face ecological disaster, which will be more dreadful than the nuclear winter. Non-violence is incomplete without voluntary curb on our extravagance. In fact non-violence and simple living and limited possession go together. Jainism finds a pattern, a rhythm and a purpose in history. The progress of civilization can not be defined in terms of material progress but in terms of moral progress. "Rome suffered a moral fall when it attained high material affluence. So did Egypt and so perhaps most countries of which we have any historical record. The descendents and kinsmen of the royal and divine Krishna too felt when they were rolling in riches". The Jainas had foreseen these dangers and therefore, had emphasised the ideal of non-possession and the practice of volunatary limitation of wants.

The Twentieth Century has been the century of Science, the 21st century will be a century of the synthesis of science and spirituality. In Jainism, science and spirituality as well as non-violence and religion meet together.

7

Multi-Dimensionality of Human Personality

Herbert Marcuse's *One-Dimensional Man* is perhaps more relevant today because of its grasp of underlying structures and tendencies of contemporary socio-economic and political development. It provides a model analysis of the synthesis of business, the state, the media, and other cultural institutions under the hegemony of corporate capital. The way that the media and politics went along with Reganism in the 1980s or Buddhism during the Gulf War or only last year during Ayodhya-episode in India indicate trends toward one-dimensional thought and politics. The resurgence of militarism and terrorism, the syndrome of denial and projection and unleashing of aggressive energies finds a mass base of approval in those who have been conditional to approve aggression. In short, one-dimensional society operates by steering erotic and destructive instinctual energies into socially controlled modes of thought and behaviour. Aggressive behaviour thus provides a social bond, unifying those who gain in power and self-esteem through identifying with forms of aggression against shared objects of hate. One-dimensional society and one-dimensional man are the results of a long historical erosion of individuality, which can be interpreted as an extended protest against the decline of individuality in advanced industrial society, the cognitive costs of which include the loss of ability to perceive another dimension of possibilities that transcend the one-dimensional thought and society. One-dimensional thought fails to distinguish between *existence* and *essence,* fact and potential and appearance and reality, and thus submits to the power of the existing society, deriving its view of the world and mode of behaviour from existing practices and modes of thought. This society is irrational as a whole. Its productivity is destructive of the free development of human needs and faculties. Hence Marcuse concludes that genuine freedom and well-being depend on liberation from the entire system of one-dimensional needs and satisfactions and require "new modes of realisation" corresponding to the new capabilities of society.[1] Freud insisted that our civilization is a repressive one. There is a conflict between the demands of our instinctive energies, explidity sexual. Freud could see no easy resolution of this antagonism, and he came to believe that in our time the possibility of simple natural love between human beings had already been abolished. But our civilization represses not only the 'instincts', not only sexuality, but any form of transcendence. Among one-dimensional men, it is not surprising that he cannot entirely deny or forget, will run the risk either of being destroyed by the others, or of betraying what he knows. A man who prefers to be dead rather than Red is normal. A man who says he has lost his soul is mad. A man who says that men are machines may be a great scientist. A man who says he is a machine is 'depersonalised' in psychiatric jargon. A man who says that Negroes are an inferior race may be widely respected. A man who says his whiteness is a form of cancer is certifiable. In short, in the context of present pervasive thinking, all our frames of reference are ambiguous and equivocal, having while propounding an existential-phenomenological foundations for a science of persons says "every man is at the same time separate from his fellows and related to them. Such separateness and relatedness are mutually necessary postulates. Personal relationness can exist only between beings who are separate but who are not isolates.[3] As such, he can live out into the world and meet others, he may have a sense of his presence in the world as a real, alive, whole, and in a temporal sense, a continuous person. Man is alone and he is related at the same time"

The super-industrial revolution thus requires a basic change in man's conception of himself, a new theory of personality that takes into account the discontinuities in men's lives, as well as the continuities, says Alvin Toffler.[4] There are the existential and the historical dichotomies in man. Men are alike, for they share the human situation and its inherent existential dichotomies; they are unique in the specific way they solve their human problem. The infinite diversities of personalities is in itself characteristic of human existence.[5]

Psychology has had its Freud, Jung, and Adler, its Erickson and Mascow, its Carl Rogers and B.F. Skinner, but it is still awaiting its Newton which will give us more adequate comprehension of human personality. By ignoring individual differences among the stars, Sir Isac could focus the attention on their behaviour or dynamics. It is tragedy that "the personality theorists have focussed either on the *structure* of an individual's personality or on *dynamics* but not both."[6] Personality does not exist in a vacuum. It has also socio-ethical-cultural dimensions apart from its biological-physiological traits. When personality is viewed from the standpoint of the ethical or the moral, it is called 'character'.[7] When we express our likes and dislikes about a person, we have the social dimension before us. Man's being can be seen from different points of view. A man without a mask is indeed very rare.[8] Everyone in some measure wears a mask. That is why the Greek word for 'persona' means a 'mask'. However the false self of the schizoid individual differs in certain important respects from the mask worn by the 'normal' person or from the hysteric.

The Physical Dimension : Differences in physique are abvious : *the pyknic,* the *athletic* and the *aesthenic.* Temperature, pressure, calorie intake, oxygen and carbon dioxide levels, all set absolute boundaries beyond which man, as presently constituted cannot venture. There are discoverable limits to the amount of change that the human organism can absorb. The level of our environment has direct physical consequences. But if we overload an environment with novelty, we get the equivalent of anxiety neurotics. True, change is not merely necessary to life; it is life. And life is adaptation. But then there are limits on adaptability. Each orientation response, each adaptive reaction exacts a price, wearing down the body's machinery bit by minute bit, until perceptible tissue damage results.

The Psychological Dimension : Psycho physiologists hold that successful adaptation can occur only when the level of stimulation is neither too law nor too high. So says Professor D.E. Berlyne of the University of Toronto : "The central nervous system of a higher animal is designed to cope with environments that produce a certain rate of stimulation...It will not perform at its best in an environment that overstresses or overloads it." Mental deterioration often began with fatigue, followed by confusion and nervous irritability and emotional exhausation. There is "bombardment of the senses", "information overload", "decision stress", confusion and uncertainty. The pathology cannot be traced neither to political doctrine or mystical core of despair or in science, technology or social change but in uncontrolled, non-selective nature of our plunge into the future.

Socio-cultural Dimension : After the family situation, there come the influences of neighbourhood, community, school, church, age mates and so on. There is social character of our thought. Just as there is a social character, there is also a 'social unconscious.' In the German Ideology, Marx wrote that "not consciousness determines life but life determines consciousness."[11] It is the social existence that determines consciousness. Rosa Luxemburg wrote in psycho analytic terminology : "The unconscious come before the conscious."[12] The consciousness of the members of the elites is a product of their social existence.[13] The relation between social character and social structure is never static, since both elements in this relationship are never-ending process. Thus, "a change in either factor means a change in both."[14]

Holistic Approach : Holistic assessment obviously reveals a great deal about a person. This may be developed into an extra-ordinary instrument for accomplishing three important purposes simultaneously : *(i)* the selection of the most suitable persons for important jobs, *(ii)* the advancement of our understanding of personality, and *(iii)* the adequate training of clinical psychologists and psychiatrists.[15] Our clinging to the absolutistic and mechanistic world view of Newton and Descartes has brought us perilously close to destruction. Fritzof Capra in his book *The Turning Point* shows how these ideas are now obsolete. Like him, we should also look forward to a new vision more consistent with the findings of modern physics. Capra's *The Tao of Physics* (London : Flamingo, Harper Collins, 3rd ed. 1991) is a holistic, system-based approach, extending to include important areas of contemporary life—medicine, psychology, economics, political science and ecology as well as physics. After discussing the five different spiritual traditions of the East, Capra finds a basic unity of the world-views, which are very much akin and fundamental to modern physics. The awareness of the unity and mutual interrelation of all things and events, the experience of all phenomena in the world as manifestations of basic oneness. All things are seen as interdependent and inseparable parts of this cosmic whole; as different manifestations of the same ultimate reality (*Ibid.*, p. 142). The basic oneness of the universe is not only the central characteristic of the mystical experience, but is also one of the most important revelations of modern physics. It becomes apparent at the atomic level and more at the sub-atomic levels. Quantum theory has abolished the notion of fundamentally separated objects. It has come to see the universe as an interconnected web of physical and mental relations whose parts are only defined through their connections to the whole.

From One-Dimensional to Multi-Dimensional Thought

In the classical Greek thought, *Reason* is sole dimension of cognitive faculty to distinguish what is true and what is false in so far as truth is primarily a condition of Being of Reality. For Socrates, epistemology is in itself ethics, and ethics is epistemology. Then comes the other dimension of thought *i.e.*, experience. With this two-dimensional thought, reason and experience, we construct two worlds—reality and appearance, truth and untruth. This divided world finds its logic in the Platonic dialectic. The two-dimensional style of thought is the inner form not only of dialectical logic but of all philosophy which comes to grips with reality. *Formal logic intended universal validity for the laws of thought because logical abstraction is also sociological abstraction.* Hence Aristotelian formal logic is sterile. Philosophic thought developed alongside and even outside this formal logic. Neither the Schoolmen nor the rationalism and empiricism of the early modern period had any reason to object to the mode of thought which had cannonised its general forms in the Aristotelian logic. The contemporary mathematical and symbolic logic is certainly very different from its classical predecessor, but they share the radical opposition to dialectical logic. Dialectical logic undoes the abstractions of formal logic and transcendental philosophy, but it also denies the concreteness of immediate experience. When experience provides the basis of logic, logical truth becomes historical truth. Instead of two-valued formalistic logic, we have today multi-valued logic, which can pave the way for a conception of multi-dimensional reality and also a multi-dimensional personality.

CONCLUSION

The one-dimensional society alters the relation between the rational and the irrational. The formerly antagonistic realms merge on technical and political ground—magic and science, life and death, joy and misery.

A man who has a sense of presence in the world as a real, alive and whole as differentiated from the rest of the world so that his identity and autonomy are never in question has inner consistency, substantiality, genuineness and worth. The one-dimensional thinking is uncritical and conformist acceptance of existing structures, norms and behaviours. One must assert his individuality and personal freedom against the technoligised status quo. Universal thinking derives its beliefs, norms, and values from existing thought and social practices, while critical thought seeks alternative modes of thought and behaviour from which it creates a standpoint of critique. One dimensional man, is bound to be uncritical, rigid and uncatholic, whereas multi-dimensionality is a creative principle and source of individual liberation and society's development. One dimensionality is a mechanics of conformity. Social change cannot be understood within the social and natural totality of human life. Man has many roles to play mostly at the same time. As a father, he has to be benefactor and disciplinarian. As a husband, he has to be loyal and considerate to his wife; as a citizen he has to serve his community and the country. Only a man who is "wholly of the present" can say something important about the present-day world, and only he who has the "most intensive and extensive consciousness" of himself and his situation can hope to be such a man. What is required is "essential thinking" (Heidiggar) or "total seeing" (*J.* Krishnamurti), or "luminous encompassive thinking" (Karl Jaspers). Multi-dimensional vision is the epistemological basis of multi-dimensional reality. Only a multi-dimensional personality can comprehend the multi-dimensional reality and adapt himself well to the multi-verse. Hence, multi-dimensional personality is an aid in the struggle for existence for a good life.

REFERENCES

1. Herbert Marcuse, *One-Dimensional Man,* London : Routlege, 1991, 2nd ed., p. 4.
2. R.D. Laing, *The Divided Self,* Preface to the Pelican Edition, 1965, p. 11.
3. *Ibid.,* p. 26.
4. Alvin Toffler, *The Future Shock,* London, Pan Books, 1970, p. 290.
5. Erich Fromm, *Man For Himself,* New York : Faweett Premier, 1975, p. 58.
6. Jameo V. Mc Connell, *Understanding Human Behaviour,* New York : Holt, Rinehart, and Winston, 3rd Ed. p., 562.

7. See N.L. Munn, *Psychology,* London : George G. Harrap, Third ed. 1956, pp. 160-61.
8. R.D. Laing, *The Divided Self,* p. 97.
9. Alvin Toffler, *Future Shock,* see chapter 15.
10. *Ibid.,* ch. 16, p. 312, *"The Physical Dimension",* pp. 296-311.
11. Preface to a contribution to the *Critique of Political Economy*.
12. Rosa Luxemburg, *Russian Revolution* and *Leninism or Marxism,* Ann Arbor, Michigan University, 1961, p. 93.
13. Erich Fromm, *Beyond the Chains of Illusion,* ABACUS, London, 1980, p. 102.
14. Erich Fromm, To *Have or To Be?* London : ABACUS, 1979, p. 134.
15. N. Munn, *Ibid.,* p. 174.

8

Reinterpreting Ahimsa for the 21st Century

This is a paradox that those who have spent fantastic money of the tax-payers over acquiring unclear stock piles have been themselves forced to find out some solution to destroy them. They realise the dread and futility of an atomic war. It seems that war has lost its dynamics. Nuclear power has not remained the monopoly of a single nation and no nation, however small or big, lives in utter isolation. The concept of geopolitics has been made redundant. The paradox is that nations aspire for peace, but they prepare for war. It seems there is maladjustment with world-psyche. Unless we find out the solution of this malaise, our life in the 21st century would be miserable. We shall not die but neither shall we be able to live with peace and happiness.

Hence before we embark upon global peace, we should learn the art of peaceful living. Non-violence is not an outward ritual, it is our life-style. The concept of nuclear preparedness, though anti-life and anti-civilization, is only the by-product of our outlook and way of thinking, created by our belief in the Doctrine of Struggle for Existence and the Survival of the Fittest. We are led to think that struggle is necessary for existence and that only a person, or a group or a country, which is the fittest—in popular vocabulary the 'mightiest' politically, economically and militarily—would be able to survive. We think that we must become powerful in order to survive and we try to cultivate more and more powers. Hence, unhealthy competition and violence become inevitable. Another reason for the growth of violence is our faith in the efficacy in the fragmentation of life. We think that there is one set of values for the individual and the family and quite another set for the society. But this is wrong. Our life is a unity and it cannot be divided into water-tight compartments called social, political or religious, etc. All act and react upon one another. Even spiritual law does not work on a field of its own. It must express itself only through the ordinary activities of life. We have not only fragmented life outside and created compartments of life and mutually opposing set of values and contradictory patterns of behaviour, we have also divided life inwardly too and developed a schizophrenic personality. Throughout, we have a fragment. Hence, we aspire for peace but plan for war; we behave as a sacrificing mother, a loving father or a husband in the family but as a man of machination and despite behaviour in politics and public life.

Hence, we lack the holistic values, which have the greatest sustaining power. The foremost of these holistic values is *love*. When love and harmony form the basis of our good family life there is no reason why it should not be the basis of society or the entire global family. The positive meaning of non-violence is Love. Literally, non-violence means absence of violence but this is one-sided and incomplete definition. Positively, non-violence means active love this is what Mahavira, Buddha, Jesus or Gandhi taught. Again, non-violence is not a static but a dynamic concept. In its dynamic condition, it does not mean meek submission to the will of the evil-doer, but it means putting of one's whole soul against the will of the tyrant and still without any ill-will against him. Ahimsa, therefore, is not "passive spirituality", it is real activity as we find in the life of Buddha and Mahavira who fearlessly carried the war of non-violent resistance into the enemy's camp and brought down an arrogant priesthood. Even Jesus, the extreme practitioner of 'resist not evil', drove out the money-changers from the temple of Jerusalem. Mahavira challenged the orthodoxy of Vedic religion and allowed women to adopt Sanyasa and prepare for salvation. He also fought the hypocrisy of those priests in giving the caste hierarchy a religious sanction. But even if Buddha, Mahavira or Jesus fought against them, they showed unmistakable love and compassion behind every act of theirs.

Non-violence or love, is not only an individual virtue, but it is a societal concept. Non-violence is not only the absence of bloodshed or murder, but it is also the absence of exploitation. Non-violence and exclusive possession can never go together. We retain our possessions on the sufferance or exploitation of the weak, immoral gains and insatiable pursuit of pleasures of the flesh. Exploitation is the essence of violence. Hence, no man could be actively non-violent and still not rise against social injustice no matter where it occurred. Non-violence is a universal principle. It is not a cloistered virtue but applicable as much to the forum and the legislatures as to the marketplace. Hence, in the 21st century, we have to make non-violence, not a matter of mere individual practice but also a matter of practice by groups and communities and nations. If it cannot be practised in all disciplines, it has no practical value. Hence, we have to show that Ahimsa is not only for the saint and seers but for the ordinary men and women living in society. It is only in a climate of non-violence that 'opposing ideologies' can peacefully co-exist. It teaches not only the respectful tolerance of other creeds and religions but also genuine appreciation of their teachings and intelligent recognition of their importance. Hence, non-violence has bigger social dimension, because it is rooted in love and friendship. But love and friendship can flourish only in a climate of equality and fraternity. "We have just enough religion to make us hate but not enough to make us love one another," Jonathan Swift once wrote. Unless we cultivate a habit of seeing beyond the horizons of our own particular faith and believe that "religious fellowship" is possible, we shall be preparing grounds for religious violence. The problem of having 'world fellowship' is impossible without world-peace and disarmament. Contemporary political thinking must be transformed and a new kind of politics to totally avert the threat of atomic doom should be created. Now, at the brink, our life depends more on worthy living. Even a hard-headed and eminent political scientist like Margenthau asserts that to think conventionally about nuclear weapons is fallacious. Then there is the problem of polymorphous, or senseless violence all over the world called terrorist violence. But this is 'irrepressible violence' and we cannot such violence by simply reciting the mantra of non-violence wipe out. Subhas Chandra Bose once wrote to Roman Rolland that non-violence cannot be at the pivot of all social action. "What must be at the centre of our concerns is the establishment of a *more just and humane social order."* If non-violence has to take roots, it must usher in a neo-polity, a new economic order and new culture. The root of violence is in the 'I' consciousness or 'ego'. The validity of which is accepted by the human race as an authority. Because of this 'ego consciousness', all our external structures and their capitalistic, socialistic, communistic symbols, are collapsing. Mahavira realised it fully well and so he asked us to purify our self with all impurities of attachment, avarice, envy etc. We cannot create a just social or economic order on the basis of 'ego' or selfishness. Selfishness is subversive of friendship and love. Hence, non-possession (*Aparigraha*) and parting away (*visarjana*) with property, assets or ownership, must form the foundation of our new economic order. It will disarm enmity, class-conflict and unhealthy competition. Either we must have a 'world economy' or face a world war. The essential of a religious revolution is its power to create goodwill. It must be relevant to the present needs of the society. Experimental verifiability is a must or else it would degenerate into orthodoxy and dogmatism. Let the *Upasana* (*devotional*) aspect be confined to devotee's wish or faith, but we must assert that the days of "personal religion" are over and we cannot enter the 21st century without the conception of a *"Universal Religion."* Similarly, the concept of national sovereignty has become outdated. But in a nuclear world, either we must live together or perish together. National boundaries are becoming irrelevant and a great stumbling block to world peace. We must strengthen the United Nations and pave the way for a *'World Government.'*

Our civilization has been passing through one of its periodic crises. In order to avert it, we need an Ahmisa-culture. We need religious idealism and co-operation, accommodation to fellowmen and tolerance. Spiritual evolution is our destiny and, therefore, the great need of the 21st century. This is what Sri Aurobindo called "a dynamic recreation of individual manhood in the spiritual type." The new society which science and technology are bringing about is a information society, a power-seeking society, which will have its own conflicts and struggles. We must remember that technology is a creation of human freedom. If technology subordinates man, it becomes anti-civilization. Hence, we have to develop a technology in harmony with the spirit of man. Similarly, growing statism and bureaucratisation must be replaced by humane administration. Today, we have a false conception of greatness, the degradation of the sentiment of justice, the idolisation of money and the lack of religious inspiration. Our civilzation has become sick also, because it does not know exactly what place to give to physical labour and to those engaged in it. All these have to be incorporated in the scheme of education. Peace-education is a must for inculcating an enduring culture of peace or Ahimsa. If the foundation of war is built in the minds of men, strategies of peace will also have to be built in our minds and hearts through education.

9

The Holistic Non-Violence in Jainism and Gandhism

It is a common misgiving that the concept of non-violence within Jainism and Gandhism is *passive* and *negative.* The worst thing is that it is regarded as a benevolent personal virtue. But it is a profound error to suppose that "whilst the law is good enough for individuals it is a not so for the masses of mankind."[1] Both the Jain Tirthankaras as well as Gandhi did not regard non-violence merely as a weapon of personal salvation but it was used as an instrument of social and cultural revolution. Hence it was bound to be social in character and also positive and dynamic in behaviour. It is true that literally the term 'non-violence' sounds negative but its meaning is highly positive". In its positive form, *ahimsa* means the largest love, greatest charity.[2] Generally, *ahimsa* is understood as non-killing of living beings but its meaning is much more comprehensive. It connotes sacrifice, love and kindness of the highest order. The positive values most akin to *ahimsa are friendliness* (*maitri*) and *compassion* (*karuna*)[3]. In *Jainism, ahimsa* is used as opposite to *himsa* (violence) which means to separate the 10 vitalities by a careless person.[4] Friendly feeling is the positive aspect of *ahimsa.* Such ideas of friendship (*maitri*), expressions of happiness and devotion, to be self-controlled and wise, equipped with knowledge, austerity and penance and dispassionate towards those who are against Jaina Dharma help in practicising *ahimsa.*

Similarly, non-violence is a dynamic virtue. In its dynamic

condition, it means "conscious" suffering. It does not mean meek submission to the will of the evil-doer but it means the putting of one's whole soul against the will of the tyrant.[5] Ours should not merely be a *'passive spirituality'* that spends itself in idle meditation on, but it should be an active thing which will carry war into the enemy's camp."[6] Lord Mahavira and Gandhi both had believed that 'never has anything been done on earth without *direct action.* They were apostles of Path of Action. So the term 'passive resistance' is insufficient as it smacks of "weakness" after all Lord Mahavira and earlier Tirthankaras from Bhagwan Rsabha to Lord Parsvanath were not mute spectators of social in justice and structural violence. They fearlessly tried to bring down on its knees an arrogant priesthood. Similarly, Christ drove out the money changers from the temple of Jerusalem and threw down curses from heaven upon the hypocrites and Pharsises.[7] Non-violence is a conscious, deliberate and extremely active force, putting restraint upon one's desire for vengeance. But vengeance is any day superior to passive, effeminate and helpless submission. Forgiveness is higher still. Vengeance too is weakness which comes out of fear of harm, imaginary or real.[8] A man who fears no one on earth would consider it troublesome even to summon up anger against one who is vainly trying to injure him. Ahimsa is the extreme limit of forgiveness.[9] But forgiveness is the quality of the brave. Ahimsa is impossible without fearlessness. Non-violence and cowardice do not go together True non-violence is an impossibility without the possession of unadulterated fearlessness.[10] He is not a follower of Mahavira, the spostle of Jainism or of Buddha or of the *Vedas,* who is afraid to die and destroys the person causing any danger to him. He is not a follower of *ahimsa* who does not care a straw if he kills a man by deceiving him in trade, or who would protect by force of arms a few cows and make away with the butcher or who, in order to do a supposed good to his country intends to satisfy one's own wants.[11]

Non-violence challenges both the frame of the mind and structure of our socio-economic life.

There are two approaches to non-violence—subjective and objective. The subjective approach is generally advocated by the religious saints and sages. According to them, peace does not dwell in outward things but within the soul. According to Jainisms five great enemies of peace inhabit within us—avarice, ambition, envy, anger and pride.[12] If these enemies were to be banished, we should enjoy perpetual peace. Hence, they hold that if we have not peace within ourselves, it is vain to seek it from outward sources. Almost all our religious teachers emphaise this subjective aspect of peace-making and hence prescribe necessary moral discipline and meditational practices. This is known as *yoga* which aims at internal peace through the cessation of mental activities.

This religious-spiritual or the subjective approach of non-violence is traditional and centuries old. Their basic tenet is that if we can change the individual, society will be automatically changed. Wars can be abolished outside, if we can reduce war-mentality within. "The Paradise is within Thee" or the "Kingdom of God" is within our own hearts and soul. As the fount of fragrance is within the musk-dear, peace is within our inner self or soul. All these look to be good in principle but it will be the height of folly and impertinence if any man conceitedly argues that it is no use renouncing the performance of certain actions but it is the internal mind alone that ought to be uncontaminated. Hence the external and the internal influence each other, and in most cases the internal psyndices the external. Thus in no case, the outward commission of Himsa without the presence of internal commission of *Himsa,* can be vindicated. He who exclusively emphasies the internal at the expense of the external targets the significance of outward behaviour.[13] Both the *Nischaya* and *Vyavahara Nayas*—the internal and external aspects—should occupy their due places.[14] Hence any one-sided and individualistic approach is unrealistic and non-holistic.

Non-violence demands a comprehensive and pragmatic supplementary approach. Firstly, we should know that non-violence is not only the negation of violence as peace is not only the absence of war. Even interpreted in the Indian context, the term non-violence (Indian equivalence of peace) seems to be of negative import of form. Non-violence is not only the absence of violence but an abundance of love even for the adversaries. Its root is not in hatred but love. So Gandhi says : "If I am a follower of *ahimsa,* I must love my enemy." Hate is the subtle form of violence. We cannot be really non-violent and yet have hate in us.[15]

It is a general misconception that non-violence and peace are meant only for saints and sages. But if we see the lives of Jain spiritual teachers, their sermons are meant for both the householders and the ascetics. The Ahimsa doctrine preached by Rsabha Deva was possibly there before the advent of the Aryans in India and the prevalent culture of the period. The institution of Sramanism grew among the imperfectly Aryanised communities of the east, spread, flourished and became highly popular and with the characteristic elasticity of Brahminism was later affiliated to the Aryan system, becoming the fourth *Ashrama.*[16] Hence, we can conclude that both Jainism and Gandhism are not more individual practice but for the practice by group and communities and nations. This shows their societal dimension. According to Gandhi, non-violence is a universal principle and its operation is not limited by a hostile environment.[17] In fact, to him, "Truth and Non-violence are no cloistered virtues but applicable as much in the forum and legislatures as in the market place."[18] Some people think that non-violence has no place in politics and worldly affairs. But Gandhi did not agree to it. He said I have no use for them as a means of individual salvation. Their introduction and application in everyday life has been my experiment all along."[19] We have to make truth and non-violence matters of practice by groups and communities and nations.[20]

(a) Domestic Non-Violence

Non-violence begins at home. Domestic violence has become a writ large phenomenon these days when children are ill-treated, wives are maltreated and often burnt and murdered, servants are treated worse than lowly animals and so on. But we practice this form of violence in our homes and our schools. "We must disarm the nursery." We must not allow toy-soldiers or gun-toys in our homes. Our homes should be the temples of peace. In Jainism, there are many prescriptions for the observance of domestic non-violence. Jainism deals a lot about the conduct of the house-holder for the observance of *Ahimsanuvrata* or vows for non-violence. The house-holder should avoid the use of wine, meat, honey, and five kinds of fruits. Drinking wine, breeds certain unhealthy passions like pride, anger, sexual desire and the like which are nothing but the different aspects of *Himsa*. Secondly, it stupifies the intellect, which sinks virtue and piety and results in the commitment of the mean and morally depraved deeds of *Himsa*. Code and conduct for observance of *ahimsa* are given in details in many books.[21] These are vows in limited forms meant for lay-man called *anu-vratees* or small vows of non-violence like abstention from gross violence (*sthula-Pranatipata-viramana*) in any form. These *anuvratas* are subdivided into seven classes—*Dik-vrata, Desa-vrata, Anartha-danda* vrata, *Sankhyaki,* Prosadho pavasa, *Upabhoqa paribhoga-Parimana* and *Athiti-Samvibhaga* with their sub-divisions. To take only one example, *Adipurana*[22] prescribes six kinds of livelihood for people (1) *Asi* (to pearn livelihood by means of using sword) (2) *Masi* (to pearn livelihood by means of writing), (3) *Krsi* (to pearn livelihood by means of agriculture) (4) *Vidya* (to earn livelihood by means of imparting knowledge) (5) *Varija* (livelihood by trade, and (6) Silpa (handicrafts etc.). There are five *bhavanas*[23] of non-violence (1) To move within a limited place in a such a way that no harm is caused to any *jiva,* (2) To give up all thoughts connected with attachment and hatred, (3) To maintain purity of meals or to control speech, (4) to take caution in taking up and laying down a thing and (5) to take food and drink in broad day light in proper time by examining it. There are also given transgressions (*Atichara*)[24] which are signals which we should not cross in order to observe the vows of non-violence (1) *Bandh* (Tying up living beings), (2) *Vadha* (Mutilation) (3) *Cheda* (beating) (4) *Ati-Bhara Niropanar* (over loading), (5) *Annopana-Nirodha* (stopping food and drink). The Jains have gone into minutest details to find out violation of the vows of non-violence in every walks of life. Hence, non-violence is not simply a matter of sermons or ideology but it is much more structural and practical.

(b) Political Non-Violence

Some people think that non-violence has no place in politics and worldly affairs. This is totally wrong. Glenn D. Paige in his book *To Non-violent Political Science* has suggested cycles of growth from violence to non-violent awakening, to exploration of non-violent alternatives and a work for global transformation. A centralised structure is bound to lead to violence and exploitation. Similarly, totalitarianism, aggressive and narrow nationalism and theocratic fundamentalism are bound to lead to violence. Political violence is rooted in absolutistic thinking. Today there is politics of power. We need a 'New World Order', in which unipolar politics and national sovereignty require alternative. We have to develop consensus politics rather than irrational Veto system in the UN Security Council. The days of nationalism are over. We must move towards a world state. In fact, nationalism has become a tribalism and anti-peace agency.

(c) Non-Violent Economics

Today, we have unbalanced development. The U.S. with a world population of only 6.5 per cent enjoys 45 per cent of world consumption, while the half of the world population is reeling under poverty, malnutrition and ill-health. This over consumption and extravagance not only leads to economic disparity but also leads to environmental pollution. Jainism and Gandhi understand this phenomenon, hence both equally stress upon the doctrine of non-possession (*Aparigraha*) and non-stealing (*Asatya*). In fact, non-violence is impossible without observing non-possession. Possession itself is a kind of violence. So Proudhan has said that property is theft. Mary has also decried the very institution of private property. But

Jainism and Gandhi go a little far and decry overconsumption. Both emphasise upon simple living. There is a new breed of consumerist culture as reflected in automation gadgetry and all that goes in the name of modernity. The pattern of urbanisation and industrialisation pursued in the west and which the ruling elite in the Third world are aping is highly resource-squandering and pollution-generating. The arrogance to control and conquer nature for trivial comforts and senseless consumerism have done great harm to the web of life and link between all living creature. Thanks to the ingenuity of the Jain saints and thinkers, who had visualised the root cause of present ecological threat and civilization crisis. They had prescribed many vows : *guna-vratas, Siksha-vratas* etc. to put a moral check upon our limitless enjoyment. If we follow even 10 per cent of these *vratas,* there will be no exploitation, no economic cut throat competition and no conflict. Gandhi had visualised the tenets of Jainism—and practised them—which form the basis of an alternative life-style, an alternative model of development and a peaceful economic order.

(d) Pedagogy of Non-Violence

The dream of a non-violent social order is impossible without a pedagogy of non-violence and peace. The present system of education neglects moral values and becomes a vested interest. Pauls Fairire has, therefore, advocated the "Pedagogy of the Oppressed". Then there is structural violence in present system of education due to regimentation, so Ivon Ellich has advocated "deschooling" or "non-formal" education. The very concept of education based on competition between man and man leads to structural violence. At present, there is education in military science in the universities and there is National Cadet Corps to train the youth in the modern warfare but there is hardly any scope for imparting peace-education, conflict-resolution and conflict prevention. We have been spending 800 billion dollars every year on amassing armaments and destructive weapons. In Jainism, non-violence is ingrained in its moral and ethical codes of conduct. There should be training in non-violence—how to control greed, fear, anger, ego, cruelty, intolerance, absolute thinking and absolute behaviour we should learn to face a violent situation and remain peaceful in face of highest provocation.

(e) Holistic Non-Violence

Non-violence cannot be achieved in a piece-meal manner. It requires a total revolution by means *(a)* transformation of the individual through moral and religious practices and *(b)* social transformation which means transformation of social, political, economic and educational order. Onesided approach has failed, as we have seen that the religious saints have been trying to bring peace on earth by trying to reform the individual but it has not yielded satisfactory results. Even there has been cruel and devastating conflict between one religion and the other. There is no conflict with the main principle that we must reform the individual before we want to reform the society. But individual lives in a society. How can we think of a non-violent man in a fully violent social order? Hence, there should be two pronged attempt—we should try to improve the individual as well as we should also reform the social order. Though, Jainism might appear to be only subjective as a religious order, but, in fact, we have seen that it is a combination of the subjective and objective elements as Gandhiji has also done.

REFERENCES

1. Gandhi, M.K., *Harijan,* 5.9.1936.
2. Gandhi, M.K., *Speeches and Writings of Mahatma Gandhi,* ed. Natesan, Madras, G.A. Natesan, p. 241.
3. Sutta *Nikaya* (MeHo Sutta), 148.
4. Umaswami, *Tattvartha Sutra,* II.13-14; VII.13.
5. *Ibid.,* VII. 2.
6. Gandhi, M.K., *Young India,* 11.8.1920.
7. Gandhi, M.K., quoted in *the Moral Challenge of Gandhi* by Dorothy Hogg, Allahabad, 1946, p.19.
8. Gandhi, M.K., *Young India,* 12.5.1920.
9. *Ibid., Young India,* 12.8.1926.

10. *Ibid., Young India,* 4.11.1926.
11. *Harijan,* 15.7.1939.
12. Natesan, *Ibid.*, p. 348.
13. *Tattvartha Sutra,* VII.5.
14. *Purusartha Siddhapaya,* Amrtachandra, Verse 50.
15. Sogam, K.C., *Ethical Doctrines in Jainism,* Sholapur : Jain Sanskriti Sangha, 1967, p. 77.
16. Dutta, *Early Buddhist* Manuscripts, London.
17. Gandhi, M.K., *Harijan,* 12.11.1938.
18. Gandhi, M.K., *Harijan,* 8.5.1937.
19. Gandhi, M.K., *Amrit Bazar Patrika,* Calcutta, 30.6.44.
20. Gandhi, M.K., *Harijan,* 2.3.40.
21. *Tattvarth Sutra of Uma Swami, Tattvartha Adhigama Bhasya,* VII. 15,16.
22. *Adi Purana,* XVII. 178-182.
23. *Tattvarthadhigama Sutra,* VII. 3. See *Tattvartha Bhasya Bhavana-Viveka,* 192-93, *Purusartha Sidhapaya,* 181.
24. *Purusartha Siddhapaya,* 183, *Tattvarthadhigama Sutra,* VII. 25, *Ratna-Karanda-Sravakachara,* 54.

10

Jainism and the War

Although apparently the Gulf War is a consequence of the most brutal and naked annexation of Kuwait by Iraq, it is basically a war for *possession* and *power*. Other explanations are more or less pretentions meant either for local consumption or for creating favourable public opinion. For example, USA who has verily championed the cause of Kuwait has been itself guilty of brazen invasion of Vietnam, Panama, Geranda and other countries in the recent past, UK and France along with Israel had invaded the Suez Canal. The Soviets had almost annexed Czechoslovakia and Hungry and had almost subjugated the entire East European countries. The Chinese did not deter to invade fellow communist country Vietnam and annex Tibet by perpetuating worst cruelty upon the most peace-loving Buddhist Lamas. However, all these aggressions or invasions do not justify Iraq's blatant occupation of Kuwait in the teeth of opposition of the world community. Iraqi overtures to link it with the Palestenian problem might be a diplomatic move to secure the sympathy of the Arabs and the Muslims in particular and the world-community in general, but it is an after-thought and without adequate moral foundation, if Iraq had felt so much for the Palestinians, instead of invading an Arab neighbour, it could have directly attacked Israel in that case perhaps there would have been no division in the Arab and Muslim world also. The other Iraqi defence of its aggression is that Kuwait had usurped much of its oil treasure through sophisticated underground technology. If it was so, there were many ways to settle it, either in the Arab League or within the framework of UNO or International Court of Justice. But Iraq did not do it, perhaps purposely in order to create an alibi. It was Kuwait which had helped Iraq with millions and billions of dollars during Iraq-Iran conflict. I think, gratitude went to the background. The last but most valid plea of Iraq for its annexation of Kuwait was that Kuwait was a part of its territory some 50 years back and it was taken away out of its country though imperialist conspiracy. Hence, it is not annexation but restoration. History is a record and register of such crimes, follies, and misfortunes of mankind. It is but the unrolled scroll of many aggressions and counter-aggressions. During the course of history, old frontiers are obliterated and new ones made, empires go down into dust to give birth to new ones. We have to accept the facts and verdict of history however unpleasant they might be. For example, we in India have to regard Pakistan and Bangladesh as fait accompli. Iraq had also recognised the independent sovereign existence of Kuwait during the past four or five decades. It was, therefore, established international political phenomenon. However, no one should have any quarrel if Iraq and Kuwait become united like the two Germanys in recent times. But forceful aggression and savage plundering of Kuwait's treasure had no justification.

However, the real motivation behind this war for both the USA led allied powers and the Iraqi ruling oligarchy is to control the Middle East politics through monopolising the oil resources. Iraq commands 16 per cent of world oil resources and Kuwait has 12.5 per cent. If Iraq could have both, it would have been in a position to dominate the oil market. The US and their allies, who depend on the oil from Middle East could not like to remain at the mercy of Iraq which had an anti-US and somewhat pro-Soviet tilt in world politics. Iraq had become a major power in the Middle East. Iran had already an anti-US stance. If both Iraq and Iran combined, it could upset the present balance of power and might have been a potential threat to Israel which is the most potent and faithful protector of US political interests in this region. If Zionist imperialism is a threat to world peace, so is Islamic fundamentalism a menace. This does not mean that Palestinian problem should not be solved. The US must come forward to settle this issue as it has hastened to come forward in the case of Iraqi invasion of Kuwait otherwise this facade of morality would be unmasked.

Now, we have to explore the dynamics of a solution and examine whether Jainism is relevant to it. Attempts have always been made to invent ways of peace. Wars have always been denounced. But unfortunately, peace and war are perennial problems/phenomena of human thought and culture. Here comes the question of means and ends. Peace is universally accepted as the ultimate and by all systems of thought. But there is radical difference among them regarding the means. Peace by means of war is impossible. As butter cannot come out of churning of water, peace cannot come out of war. Peace can be established only by means of peace. Unless we learn to reorganise our daily life on the basis of non-violence, world peace will be only an illusion. Inspired by the precepts of the Bible "Thou shall not kill", Christian pacifism had developed into not playing the role of an armed soldier as "Conscience objector" while employing all possible means to check war and remove inequality of all kinds, exploitation and injustice. Round about A.D. 300 we have examples of men punished for refusing, when required, to serve as soldiers : the best known is that of Maximillian martyred in North Africa in A.D. 295. However, with all its emphasis on non-violence, we do not find a single instance in the history of Jainism when a responsible member of the Jain laity refused to play the role of an armed soldier. However, when Gandhiji taught us the way of unarmed resistance (*Satyagraha*) which required consumate courage and enterprise but no physical power, the Jainas have willingly taken part in all Gandhian non-violent movements.

However, this principle of pacifism and non-violence cannot be actualised by verbal discussions an sympathies or by practising rituals of feedings ants or by only practising vegetarianism or meal before dust, etc. In order to realise non-violence is to practise the vow of absolute non-possession or limited possession of property or as Gandhi said, trusteeship and by leading a life full of simplicity. Non-violence is unthinkable without non-possession or limited possession, which in turn is impossible without voluntary curtailment of our necessities of life. In fact, possession of property lies at the root of the world-crisis. Greed is the root of possessive instinct. Without voluntary control of this passion of greed there is no hope of freedom—individual, social or national. On account of this uncontrolled greed there is perpetual fear of conflict and war, internal as well as international. This is at the root of the present gulf-crisis. Unless, Jainism can provide practical non-violent way of carrying out the vow of limited possession of property and regulate life accordingly, it is only an arm-chair philosophy.

Besides the vicious doctrine of possession, the concept of power is very fundamental in the context of world-politics. The concept of power is as fundamental to politics as energy is to physics. The progress of science and technology during the last two hundred years has no doubt released tremendous forces of production and organisation giving comfort and entertainment, knowledge and culture, peace and security within the potential reach of every man, woman and child in the world, but it has also made the modern state more powerful than the leviathan, with the result that those who have usurped the state power, they behave like dictators—Hitler, Mussolini, Saddam or Bush. Therefore, we are confronted today by an overwhelming paradox of poverty amidst plenty, darkness in the midst of untold facilities of enlightenment. Hence, war, armament and Machiavellian diplomacy are not isolable phenomena. Immediate motives and occasions apart, they represent a method of pressing claims, a way of resolving disputes; in short, an instrument of policy natural to schemes of things which admit the validity of violence. If disputes of Iraq and Kuwait, for instance, are being settled on the plane of brutal force, it is because social life has been moving on the corresponding planes of hatred, frustration and exploitation. They have permeated international relationships, internal literature and outlook so deeply. Force and fraud still have got social sanction. Hence, a tremendous effort, rational and moral, is needed to bring home the truth to the world that a way out of the present strife into universal peace and welfare lies in revising human relationships so as to substitute the principle of *non-violence* for violence, force and war. In internal affairs, we must remember that the systems of caste and class rest in ultimate analysis partly on force and make-believe and partly on tradition and orthodox beliefs. Hence, Lord Mahavira had rebelled against caste-system and had brought women on equal footing. In short, the principle of non-violence really means that equal regard be paid to the welfare of all men and women. It requires wholesale transformation in the internal government of states and a new arrangement in socio-economic life based on maximum decentralisation, virtue, morality in harmony and organic vitality. When the whole social fabric is based on force, sympathy and mutual aid, affection and love become the worst casualties. For a non-violent world without war, we need a non-violent politics, a non-violent economics, a non-violent social order and last but not the least a non-violent education and a culture of non-violence. It is wrong to hold that human relationship are based entirely on force. Human society simply could not endure in such an environment. A great deal of sympathy and mutual help, sacrifice and service have always gone to the making of the family, wider associations and of the community as a whole.

As we have said earlier, non-violence and non-possession go together. Possession implies attachment and unrestraint. What is needed is a certain self-restraint in the face of pleasures, a certain stoicism before temptations, a certain detachment from superfluities and super-abundances. Ruthless and lustful competition for wealth and empire is the bane of the present age and is responsible for a crisis like the Gulf-War. This is the negation of sordid, all-absorbing materialism. The Gulf oil has spawned superfluities around. This has resulted in a life which appropriates the labour of others without one doing any kind of manual work for the production of the daily necessities in spite of the capacity to do so. The Western life is also that of uncontrolled competition, aggressive nationalism, economic imperialism, exploitation of the weak and racial pride.

In fact, a crisis like the Gulf-War is only the symptom, not the cause of the world-crises. In order to banish such wars, we have to banish the culture of violence and possession. Non-violence is the first necessity of life. Nuclearism is bound to push the mankind either to non-violence or to non-existence. Similarly, unbriddled desire for material pleasures is bound to cause dangerous depletion of non-renewable sources of energy, rape of the earth and first rate environmental crisis on an unprecedented scale that might prove more catastrophic than nuclear disaster. Besides, it will lead to competition, strife and war. Thus, acceptance of non-violence and non-possession as the guiding principles of life is the only way out. And this underlines the relevance of Jainism in the modern world.

The Gulf-War was also the result of hard-headedness and absolutistic attitude of mind. Both the parties think that they alone are right. However, Iraq's attitude was more rigid and absolutistic. It has most brazenly defied the request of the world body, in which not only the Anglo-American powers but also the two other non-Anglo-US powers, the USSR and China, were parties, notwithstanding some of the important Arab and Muslim countries like Egypt, Syria, Pakistan and Saudi Arabia. Hence it was a one-sided approach. Iraq would have earned the goodwill of the world had it shown preparendness to accept either UN Secretary General's Peace Plan or abide by any arbitration or mediation. By not doing so, Iraq has unwittingly divided the Arab and Muslim world and has given the opportunity to US army to come to the Middle East. The result of this absolutistic way of thinking is the destruction of Iraq and untold miseries to millions of its people.

Let us hope, the Gulf-War will provide us a lesson that war is no solution to any problem. Violence has no end. Greed has no boundary. Absolutism in thought is no sign of cultured life. The Jain culture is Catholic and non-absolutistic in word, deed and thought and hence it is most relevant today.

11

The Contribution of Haribhadra to the Yoga-Vidya

I

The Indian systems of thought and culture are not mere speculations on the external nature of things but also of the mysteries of our mind and soul. Even frankly realistic disciplines like Jainism, Nyaya-Vaisesikas and the Himansakas show most serious concern to fathom the depths of mind and unravel the mysteries of spirit. The common channels and sources of knowledge like perception, inference etc are found to be inadequate and it has been the abiding spiritual ambition of man to extend the frontiers of his knowledge. Even to a scientist, any attempt to put a limit to our knowledge is the result of some wrong notions. Nothing is regarded as static or absolute. Even to the Marxists, "there is nothing in the nature which cannot be explained". Thus the growth of human knowledge has been a sort of progressive limitation of sceptical and agnestic attitudes. It seems that it can extend without assignable limits to knowledge of mankind.[1] A spiritual conviction and a constant urge for the ultimate truth is the mane of our common Sadhana. It is not only the perfection of the cognitive faculty of the Self but also it ultimate end.[2] Hence "Know Thyself" (*atmanam Biddhi*) has been regarded as the climax of our spiritual *Sadhana*. There are obvious limitations to our sensory knowledge, there are antinomies of reasons. Hence, we have to transcend these usual sources of knowledge in order to realise the truth. This process has a common term in Indian thought—Yoga. It is not against but beyond reason (*Jnana Vignam Sahitam*).

II

The terra *Yoga* symbolises the core of Indian Spiritual *Sadhana*. The four-fold social divisions of occupation (*varna-vibhajana*), its trade and business, language and physical culture etc. are only the external signs of the Aryans;[3] even the concept of other world (heaven-hell) is not its essential ingradients.[4] Its real and inner spirit lies in the absolute concentration of thought or one pointedness on the ultimate reality which is beyond the present space and time.[5] Perhaps, on account of this distinctive feature, the Aryans have been judged as superior to all other races and climes.

In life, theory and practice, knowledge and action, empirical and the transcendental require a synthesis. As a matter of fact, the real practice of one's knowledge is called *yoga*. Knowledge precedes, yoga succeeds. But a knowledge without its practice or implementation is not only incomplete but also ambiguous. Thus *Yoga* is superior to the *tanas, jnana,* and *karma*.[6] It is the best of all the three and includes devotion also. Yoga or union with God which is attained through *bhakti* is the highest spiritual goal Jnana is scriptural learning (*Sastra panditya*)[7] and not spiritual realization. Truly wise men is the *Yogi*. Without Yoga or concentration of mind, the human energies are frittered away in many directions and go waste. Hence, the spirit of man is the key for the success of all practical activities. A man versed only in scriptural learning but lacking in yogic realisation is called as "the friend of the learned"[8] but not a yogi.

Then there are two dimensions of yoga—the external and the internal. Even the process of concentration is regarded its outer frame, where as renunciation of all attachment and reducing oneself to zero is its inner spirit. The real yoga, therefore, consists in the inner poise, self-mastery, its conquest of anger, sensitiveness, pride and ambitions.[9] So there are two types of yoga—the yoga of knowledge and the yoga of Action. The former consists in the knowledge about the Self, its bondage, liberation and the path of liberation. But mere knowledge or theoretical knowledge is no good. What is more important is the performance of work without any selfish attachment to results, with a view to securing the welfare of the world, with the realization that agency belongs to the modes of *Prakriti* or to God himself.[10] In fact, Yoga consists in practical realization of the Self.

There are three-fold traditions of Yoga—literature in Indological writings—the Vaidika, the Jaina, and the Buddha. Though the term *'yoga'* has occurred many times in Rg-Veda, it has always been used in the sense of "Union" only and never in the sense of meditation or concentration of mind. Even such key words of the yoga literature like meditation, non-attachment breath control, withdrawal from external world etc. are absent in the *Rg-Veda*.[11] However, the Upanisads[12] do abound in the mention of these concepts. There might be differences of opinion regarding the nature or number of the ultimate reality but there is a remarkable unanimity regarding the acceptance of yogic Sadhana for its realization. All the Vedic systems including the Nyaya[13]-Vaisesika,[14] Sankhya[15]-Yoga,[16] and Vedanta[17] accept the utility and relevance of Yoga in their respective systems. Purva-Mimansa is the only exception which does not ever refer to yoga. It is interested in ritualistic action. The Gita[18] and the Mahabharat,[19] the Bhagavata[20], the Yoga Vasistha[21] and the important-works on Tantra[22] including many works of *Hatha-Yoga* accept the place and importance of yoga. Many medieval saints and scholars like Jnana-deva[23] Ambeya,[24] Kabir[25] etc. have discussed the subject of yoga with great seriousness.

III

Together with its tradition, the term Yoga has a chequered history. In the Rg Veda, it is used in the sense of "union", later on in about 700-800 B.C., it is used in the sense of 'yoking a horse' (uncontrolled spiritual horses). It can be traced also in

German-Joch, OE-Geoc, Latin-Jugum Greek-Zugon.[26] In Panini's time, the term 'yoga' had attained its technical meaning of concentration. In Jainism, the tens *Carita* (conduct) is the exact equivalent of the general term 'yoga'.[27] Jaina tradition, predominantly being ascetic and world-negating lays stress upon wilful silence (*mauna*), austerities (*tapas*), and other yogic activities. The Jaina *Agamas* describing about the *conduct of the Sadhus (Sadhucharya)* refer to many yogic activities like the abstenations and observances (*Yama* and *Niyama*), study (*swadhyaya*), austerities (*tapas*), withdrawal of the senses (Pratyahara) etc.[28] Even the acts of volition (*Pravritti*) has to be surcharged by the spirit of volition in the negative sense (*nivritti*), technically called as *Asta, Pravachana-Mata.*[29] Jaina Sadhus are directed to concentrate on study and meditation for the three fourths of daily routine.[30] In the Jaina *Agamas*[31] and the *Niryuktis,*[32] the term 'yoga' has been mostly used in the sense of concentration of mind with numerous classifications and sub-classifications. Even Tattvartha[33] refers to *dhyana* and the *Dhyana-Sataka* of Jinabhadra Gani Kshma Sraman is only explication of the nation of *dhyana*. Hence, yoga has been rooted in the Aganeic tradition.

IV

But it was Haribhadra who for the first time gave an altogether new dimension in the Interpretation of Yoga. It is only Haribhadra who defined the term 'yoga' in the sense of "what leads one to emancipation" (*mukhena jeyano jago savvo vi dhammovavaro*).[34] Thus he has ushered a new era in the yoga literature of the Jainas. He wrote important yoga treatises like *yoga-bindu, yoga-dristi-Sammuchaya, yoga-Vimsika, Yoga-Sataka* and *Sodasaka*. The term yoga was used in the general sense of subduing the senses and the mind and the process of concentration and ecstasy even in the earlier stages of the Jaina thought as well as the early Buddhist thought. But the terms Jnana (*dhyana*) and *Samadhi* were more in vogue than the term yoga. It is only in the *yoga-sutra* of Panini that we find the proper location of *dhyana* in the eightfold process of yoga, for the first time.[35] Haribhadra's in his characteristic outlook did not discuss and interpret yoga according to the Jaina tradition only but he made a comparative and critical study of Patanjali's yoga[36] etc. The description of eightfold standpoints[37] in the *Yoga-dristi-Sammuchaya* is altogether a new dimension in yoga literature.

All spiritual and religious activities that lead towards emancipation are considered by Haribhadra as yoga. His Ingenuity lies in the yogic interpretation of the Jaina doctrine of Spiritual development (*Ganasthana*). The soul has inherent capacity for emancipation but this capacity remains dormant and inactive due to Karmic influences. But the soul can be roused to active spiritual excertion which is nothing other than yogic activities. The Jainas do not believe either in the eternal revelation of the truth like the Mimansakas and the Vedantins or, in its revelation by a Supreme Divinity like the Niyaya-Vaisesikas and the Patanjali Yoga. Only rare souls known as *tirthankaras,* who have acquired potency of revealing the truth and preaching it to the world by their moral and virtuous activities can also help in arousing us from moral slumber. The centrifugal tendency of soul to run away from the fetters of world existence is thwarted by a centripetal force of attachment (*raga*), repulsion (*devesa*),[38] and perverted attitude (*mithyattva*). However, the soul, when it achieves purification feel uneasiness with the worldly existence and shows manifestation of energy known as *Yathapravrttakarana* for the spiritual advancement. But the struggle between the two-fold processes, centrifugal and the centripetal[39] continues unless the soul develops such spiritual strength as is destined to lead it to final emancipation by reducing the duration and intensity and also the mass of Karmic-matter through the triple processes of *Yathapravrttakarana, apurvakarana, and anivrttikarna.*[40] The soul then starts climbing up the spiritual ladders of *Upasamasreni* (ladder of subsidence) and *Ksapakasreni* (ladder of annihilation) upto the final fourteenth stage of absolute motionlessness.

Haribhadra's style of describing the fourteen stages of spiritual development through the process of yoga is original and illuminating. While discussing, he has mentioned the names of many yogis[41] and treatises on Yoga.[42] A crucial problem is posed by Haribhadra to know the real point of the beginning of the spiritual development of soul desiring salvation in the timeless world of attachment. According to Haribhadra, when the Influence of deluding Karma start decreasing, the process of spiritual development starts. The state prior to this beginning, of the spiritual development is called *Acharam Pudgal Paravarta,* while the posterior state is called *charam Pudgala Parvarta*. Between these two poles of *Acharam* and *Charam,* we have the different stages of spiritual development.[43] Here in the process of yoga begins, which causes simplicity, humility, catholicity, benevolence and other virtues in the soul. The emergence of these ethical virtues are the outer signs of the spiritual development of the soul.

The special feature of Haribhadra is his comparative studies in yoga. For example, in *yogavimsika,* where in five kinds of activities (*Sthana, Urna, artha, alambana* and *analambana*) divided into external activity (*karma-yoga*) and Internal spiritual activity (*Jnanayoga*),[45] are discussed, Haribhadra has tried to correlate them with stages of Spiritual development (*Ganasthana*). For example, these activities can be properly practised only by those who have attained the 5th or a still higher stage of *Gunasthana*. In this way, Haribhadra correlates the different stages of *Gunasthanas* to the different stages of concentration (*dhyana*).[46] Haribhadra compares *analambana yoga* with *Samprajnata Samadhi* in Patanjali's system,[47] the final consumation of *analambana* concentration is *Asamprajnata Samadhi*. Similarly the fourteenth stage of spiritual development corresponds to the *dharmamegha Samadhi* of Patanjali's system, to *amrtatman* of yet another system, to *bhavasatru* of a third system, to *Sivodaya* of yet another, to *Sattvananda* of yet others and to *para* of yet another school.[48] Similarly, Haribhadra tries to show the unanimity of the conception of final self-realization of all the systems of thought. Haribhadra enumerates eight primary defects,[49] from which the mind of a *yogin* must always be free. By practicing the concentration of mind the soul realizes itself. This is known as Supreme bliss (*Parmananda*) in the Vedanta, the extinguished lamp (*vidhmatadipa*) of the Buddhists, extinction of animality (*pasutvavigama*), end of suffering (*dukkhanta*), freedom from the specific qualities (*Nyaya-Vaisesika*), and detachment from the elements (*bhutavigama*).[50] Like an impartial truth-seeker, Haribhadra asks the seekers to keep their minds open and investigate the truth with perfect detachment and freedom from prejudices.

Similarly, Haribhadra shows that there is a fundamental unity among all apparently conflicting systems of thought regarding the means to free from the worldly existence. He asks us to see unity in diversities. He lays down five steps as a complete course of yoga : contemplation of truth (*adhyatma*), repeated practice (*bhavana*), concentration of mind (*dhyana*), equanimity (*samata*) and annihilation of all the traces of Karman (*Vrittisamksaya*).[51] The same principle, according to Haribhadra, is expressed by different terms. It is *Purusa* in the Vedanta as well as the Jaina system, as *Jnana* in the Buddhist school, *ksetravit* in the Samkhya system. Similarly, the fundamental ground of worldly existence is called *avidya* (*vedanta* and *Buddhism*), Prakrti (*Sankhya*), Karman (*Jainas*). Similarly, the relation between matter and spirit is known as bhranti (*vedanta* and *Buddhism*), *Prvrtti* (*Sankhya*) and *bandh* in Jaina system.[52] Haribhadra referring to Gopendra of the Sankhya System holds that the Purusa does not even enquire about the path of realisation unless the *Prakrti* has turned her face from it. In other words, it is the nature of the Spirit to get disentangled from matter. For this requisite purification of the soul is very necessary. Then the soul becomes a *bodhisattva* or *tirthankaras*.[53] When a man becomes a *boddhisattva*, there is no mere spiritual degeneration to him.[54] He does not commit evil or sin, on the contrary, he is keen in exclusively in the well-being of others, acquires wisdom, treads upon right path and appreciates merit.[55] Haribhadra compares the Jaina conception of Tirthankaras with the Boddhisattvas. He distinguishes three categories of souls destined to be emancipated—Tirthankaras,[57]

Ganadharas[58] and Munda Kevalins.[59] Haribhadra's contribution also lies in suggesting five-fold stages of preliminary preparation for yoga as we find in Patanjali's scheme of *Yama* and *Niyama*. As we have referred earlier, the stages of the soul are *adhyatma*,[60] *bhavana*,[61] *dhyana, Samata*[62] and the last *Vrttisamksaya*.[63] Here the accumulated and obscuring karmas are destroyed for ever and the soul attains omniscience[64]. and final emancipation.

In *Yogadrstisammuchaya*,[65] Haribhadra presents a novel plan of classification of yogic stages. The core of this scheme is the concept of *Drsti* which means attitude towards truth. The most important feature of spiritual development is acquisition of love of truth (*Samyagdrsti*). The gradual purification of its love of truth takes place corresponding to the purification of soul. So long the soul has not cut the knot and attained purification, our attitude is bound to be wrong, and perverse called as *avidya, mithyatva* or *darsanamoha*. Without purification of the soul, we can have only common place attitude (*oghadrsti*) as opposed to right attitude (*sad-drsti*) or attitude of the spiritually advanced soul (*yoga-drsti*). Haribhadra listed eight kinds[66] of gradual development of love of truth (*drsti*) corresponding to the eight-fold stages of Patanjail's yoga. Haribhadra refers to the consensus of opinion of a number of authors regarding the stages of yoga in his *Sopajnavrtti*.[67] His love of truth is so great that he can never be sectarian. Haribhadra asks us to realise the truth by means of all the three organs—scripture, logic and practice of yoga in keeping with the best tried and trusted tradition of India. The truth is one. It cannot be many. There is only the difference of angles or terminology. Yoga is not the monopoly of a particular sect or system. It is based on direct experience of the seers and lovers of truth. Differences in terminologies of different system about the same concept is illustrated by Haribhadra. For example, the state of final realisation is known as *Sadasiva* in one system, *Parabrahmana* in another, *Siddhantatman* in the third and *tathata* in another system.[68] Hence, there can be no conflict when the truth is realised. Controversies take place only when the truth has not been realized[69] as an empty pot sounds much. The various revelations have to be understood from various contexts and angles. The love of truth (*drstis*) give us the power to cultivate faith in spiritual revelations. Similarly, referring to the seventh drsti (*Prabha*), Haribhadra compares it with *Visabhagsa-Pariksaya* in the Buddhist School. *Prasantavahita* in the Sankhya system and *Sivavartman* in the Srivavartman, and as *dhurvadhvan* in the *Mahavartikas*.[70]

Besides eight-fold *drstis* corresponding to the eight steps of yogic sadhana in Patanjali, Haribhadra refers to the three-fold yoga—The first stage is *Iccha Yoga*, when in spite of knowledge and will, the yogic practitioner falters in his practice on account of enertia (*Pramada*).[71] The second stage is called *Sastra Yoga*,[72] wherein the practitioner does never falter in his yogic practices, strictly follows the scriptural injunctions and has developed penetrating insight. The third and the last stage of yoga is *Samarthya Yoga*,[73] when he has fully mastered the scriptural injunctions.

REFERENCES

1. Singh, Ramjee, *The Concept of Omniscience in Ancient Hindu Thought*, Delhi : Oriental Publisher. 1979, p. 336.
2. *Ibid.*, *The Jaina Concept of Omniscience*, Ahmedabad : L.D. Institute of Idology, 1974, p. 221.
3. Max Muller, *Biographies of Words and the Home of the Aryans*, p. 50.
4. *Bhagavad Gita*, IX.21, "They return to the world of mortals when their merit is exhausted".
5. Max Muller, *Sacred Books of the East*, Vol. I, p. 23 (Introd.)
6. *Bhagavad Gita*, VI. 46.
7. B.G. (*Sankar Bhasya*), VI. 46.
8. *Yoga-Vasistha*, Nirvana Prakarana, ch. 21.
9. *Bhagavad Gita*, II, 48.
10. B.G., III. 43 (View of Yamunacharya in *Gitartha Samgraha*).
11. The term *yoga* has occurred many times in the RgVeda, I.34.9; X.266.5; I.18.7; I.5.3; II.8.1; IX.58.3.

12. *Tatittiryopnisad.* II.4; *Katha,* II.6. II; *Sveta Svatara* II. II, IV. 3 ; I.14; *Chhandogya,* VII.6.1; VII.6.2; VII.7.1; VII.26.1.

13. *Nyaya-Sutra* of Gotama, I.1.1; IV.2.38; IV.2.42; IV.2.46.

14. *Vaisesika-Sutra* of Kanada, I.1.4; VI.2.2; VI.2.8.

15. *Sankhya-Sutra* of Kapila, I.1; III.30; III.31; III. 32 III.33; III.34.

16. *Yoga-Sutra* of Patanjali, IV.33.

17. *Brahma-Sutra* of Badarayana, 3rd. chapter is known as *Sadhana Pada.*

18 The first six chapters deal with Karma Yoga, middle six to the Bhakti Yoga and the last six deal with Jnana-Yoga.

19. *Mahabharat,* Santi Parva, 193,217,246,254 chaps. Anugasasna Parva, 36, 246 etc.

20. *Srimad Bhagavat Mahapurana,* Skandha III, ch.28; XI. 15, 19, 20 etc.

21. *Yoga Vasistha,* chapters on Vairagya, Mumukshu-Vyabhara, Utapatti, Sthiti Upasana and Nirvana.

22. *Mahanirvana Tantra,* 3rd chap.

23. *Jnaneshwari,* 6th chapter.

24. *Sidhanta-Samhita* of the Suhiroba Ambiya.

25. Kabir's *Bijaka* is an important treatise on Yoga Mysticism.

26. Das Gupta, S.N., *Philosophical Essays,* Calcutta University, 1941, p. 179.

27. *Ibid.*, *History of Indian Philosophy,* Vol. I, p. 226,

28. Sanghvi, S., *Darshan Aur Chintan,* Ahmedabad, Gujrat Vidya Sabha 1957, p. 45.

29. *Uttardhyana Sutra,* chap. 24

30. *Ibid.,* ch. 26.

31. *Sthananga,* IV.1; *Samvayang* IV; *Bhagvati* XXV.7; *Uttaradhyana,* XXX.35.

32. *Avashyak Niryukti* (Kayotsarga) Gatha 1462-1486.

33. Umaswami, *Tattvartha Sutra,* IX.7.

34. Haribhadra, *Yoga Vimsika,* Karika, I.

35. Tatia N.M., *Studies in Jaina Philosophy,* Varanasi : Jaina Cultural Research Society, 1951, p. 261.

36. Haribhadra, *Yoga-bindu*, 418, 420.
37. Haribhadra, *Yoga-dristi-Sammuchaya*, Karika, 13.
38. *Visesa Vasyaka-Bhasya*, Yajovijaya Jaina Granthamala No. 35, G. 1194.
39. *Ibid.*, Gatha 1204-1217.
40. *Tattvartha Raj Vartika* of Bhatta Aklanka, Kashi, 1935, p. 327; *Labhdhisara of Nemichandra*, R.J.S. No. 8, Nirnaya Sagar Press, 1916, 35.
41. *Gopendra* (*Yoga-bindu*, verse-200), Kalatita (*yoga-bindu*, verse-300) Patanjali, Bhadanta Bhaskarbandhu, Bhagvadanta Vadi (*yoga-dristi-Sammuchaya*-Verse-16—Tika).
42. *Yoga-nirnaya* (*yoga-dristi-sammuchaya*, verse 1 Tika).
43. *Muktyadvesa-dvatrimsika*, Verse-28.
44. Sanghvi, *Ibid.*, p. 264.
45. Haribhadra, *Yoga-Vimsika*, I. 2; *Sodasaka-Prakarana* of Haribhadra with Yasobhadra's commentary, Jamnagar, 1992, XIII.4; XIV.I.
46. *Yoga-Vimsika*, I., 18.
47. *Ibid.*, 20.
48. *Yaso-Vijyas* Tika on Yoga-Vimsika of Haribhadra, 20; *Yoga-bindu* of Haribhadra, Ahmedabad : Jaina Granthamala Prakashaka Sabha Series No. 25, 1940, 422.
49. *Sodasaka-Prakarana* of Haribhadra with Yasobhadra's Tika, XIV. 2-3; XVI.14.
50. *Ibid.*, XVI.1-4.
51. *Yoga-Bindu*, 17-18 (with *Sopajnavrtti*).
52. *Yoga-bindu* of Haribhadra with *Svopjna Vritti*, 17-18.
53. *Ibid.*, 270.
54. *Ibid.*, 271.
55. *Ibid.*, 272.
56. *Ibid.*, 274.
57. *Ibid.*, 284-8.
58. *Ibid.*, 289.
59. *Ibid.*, 290.

60. *Yoga-bindu* of Haribhadra with *Svopjna Vritti,* 17 18, 358-59.

61. *Ibid.,* 360-61.

62. *Ibid.,* 364-65.

63. *Ibid.,* 31.

64. *Ibid.,* 366-67.

65. *Yogadrsti Sammuchaya* of Haribhadra, ed. Prof. L. Suali, Ahmedabad, 1912, 12.

66. The eight love of truth (drstis) are—1. *Mitra* (YDS 22, 22-40), 2. *Tara* (YDS 41-48), 3. *Bala* (YDS 49-50), 4. *Dipra* (YDS 57-58), 5. *Sthira* (YDS, 152-4), 6. *Kanta* (YDS 160-62), 7. *Prabha* (YDS 168-69), 8. *Para* (YDS 179, 184).

67. *Ibid.,* 16.

68. *Yogadrsti Sammuchaya....* 157,128.

69. *Ibid.,* 130.

70. *Ibid.,* 173-74.

71. *Ibid.,* 3.

72. *Ibid.,* 4.

73. *Ibid.,* 5.

12

Contribution of the Jaina Agamas to Indian Culture

1. The Place of the Agamas in Cultural History of India

Language and Literature apart from art and architecture constitute the most important records of the cultural history of a country. Hence, the study of the Agamas is bound to reveal the most important observations of Jainism and its contribution to Indian culture.

As we all know, the collective term given by the Jainas to their Sacred Literature is called Agamas written in Prakrit just as the Buddhist Pitakas in Pali and the Brahmanical Vedas in Sanskrit. The Jaina Agamas like the Buddhist Pitakas contain the sermons of their founders. They were later on codified by their trusted disciples into the language of the people just for the larger benefit of the masses. Thus the original Sacred Books of both the Jainas and the Buddhists were written in Prakrit, *i.e.* Ardhamagadhi and Pali respectively. Being missionaries, their mission was to interest not only the intellectuals but the common people and hence they used the language of the common man. The Jaina Agamas accord a very respectable position to Ardha-Magadhi by calling it not only the language of the Aryans[1] but also of the celestial gods[2]. The Buddhist Tripitakas enjoin upon their followers to use the local dialect of the people[3] for the propagation of their sacred teachings. This was nothing but a legitimate protest against the touch-me-not attitude of the vedic scholars who would never descend down from their ivory tower of Sanskrit language and on the other hand they would look down upon the use of these languages of the people for imparting religious instructions. Prakrit and Pali were declared to be the languages of the outcastes or Mlechhas.[4] This shows their regard for maintaining the so-called cultural purity by the priestly order to ensure their monopoly for ever. To be impartial, we can not deny that there was some amount of animosity among the Jainas and the Buddhist scholars against the use of Sanskrit language at least at the critical stages which is amply reflected in the painful sight of some of Pali and Prakrit scholars maintaining linguistic isolationism as a result of which they remained unaware of the Indian heritage as depicted in Sanskrit language and literature. The Bhikkhus of the Hinayana cults of Buddhism in Burma and Ceylon are examples of such isolationism. Similarly, many eminent scholars of Sanskrit of that age remained unaware of the growth and development of ideas in the field of Pali and Prakrit languages. The cause of this linguistic animosity was also unhealthy religious rivalries which are de-mostrated into the literature of the 7th and 8th Centuries A.D. All these factors went to retard the growth of cultural synthesis in India at least for some time.

In this respect, the Jaina tradition has been rather liberal. Down from the days of Arya Rakshit (2nd Century of Vikram Samvat) and Uma Swami (3rd Century of V.S), there has been equal interest in Prakrit and Sanskrit so much so that both these languages became the common and combined treasures of the Jaina. Nay, the Jainas have adopted other regional languages also like Kanada and Tamil in South India, Gujarati and Marathi in Western India and even Hindi in Central India for the propagation of their religious teachings or literary pursuits.

II

Pt. Sukhalalji[5] has divided the entire extent of Jaina philosophical literature broadly into four periods beginning with the Agamic period. Notwithstanding the differences in the two traditions of Dig-ambaras and Svetambaras, the Jainas generally agree that the Agamas constitute the inspired wisdom of Lord Mahavira,[8] when he attained perfection and Omniscience. The sermons were later on codified by his chief disciples called Ganadharas. According to the Jaina tradition, there are only two types of persons, who are qualified to know the secrets of religion—the-Omniscient (Kevalin) who directly perceive everything of all places and of all times. Then there is another class of persons who understand the meaning and significance of sermons indirectly *i.e.* through the lectures or sermons by the Kevalins themselves. They are called *Sruta Kevalins*. Acharya Yati Vrsabha has given the chronological account of the Missionary (Acharya) tradition of 683 years after the Nirvana of Lord Mahavira having 3 Kevalins, 5 Sruta Kevalins, 20 different orders of Acharyas.[7]

According to the Svetambara tradition,[8] the last compilation of the Agamas had been done at Valabhi after 980 years of the death of Lord Mahavira at the time of Devardhi, however the compilations of some of the Agamas were done at Patliputra also which was after 250 years of Lord Mahavira's death. The Agamic literature is vast and stupendous, comprising of Twelve Angas, 12 Upanagas, 4 Mulas, 2 Chulikas Suttras, 6 Cheda Suttras, 10 Prakirnakas etc.[9] The commentation on these Agamas are called *Niryuktis* and *Bhasyas* which are in prose style and in poetry style they are called *Churnis*. Available Niryuktis are said to be compositions of Bhadrabahu, the Second, which contain subtle philosophical discussions on the problems of existence of soul, analysis of knowledge and meaning etc. The *Bhasyas* contain the fuller accounts of all subjects. Sanghadas Gani and Jinabhadra are the two famous Bhasyakaras. Jinabhadra was a versatile genius, who has written practically on all subjects under the sun. Sanghadas Gani has limited himself to the task of dealing with the problems of epistemology and the ethics of the Jaina Sadhus. Among the Churnikaras, Jinadas Mahattara is a notable figure. Churnis are shorter commentaries in prose on the pattern of Jatakas. In Sanskrit, the oldest commentaries of the Agamas is of Acharya Haribhadra (757-857 V.S.), next to whom are Shilanka Suri (8th Cent V.S.) and Sangacharya, Abhayadeva and Malladhari Hema Chandra and last but not the least Malayagiri. All these scholars wrote their commentaries in Sanskrit and Prakrit but they were so vast and deep that shorter commentaries in the languages of the people was considered essential. Hence, we find the composition of many *Primers* and *Beginners* in regional languages like *Taba* in *Gujarati.* Acharya Dharma Singh is said to be an important author of such *Beginners* and *Primers.*[10]

According to the Digambara tradition[11], all the old Agamas are said to have lost except the 12th called *Dristivada.* They regard Bhadrabahu as the last *Sruta Kevali,* with him out of 14 Purvas, 4 were lost. After Bhadrabahu, the different Acharyas became the teachers of 11 Angas and 10 Purvas and the process of disintegration continued up till 683 years after Mahavira's Nirvana. An important Acharya, named Dharasena initiated his two most able disciples, named, Puspadanta and Bhutabali into the Agamas, who later on compiled the Sermons in the form of a monumental epics of religion called, Sat-Khandagama in Prakrit. A contemporary of Acharya Gunabhara compiled *Kasaya-Pahuda* upon which Yati Brasabha wrote a commentary in Prakrit after he learnt it from Arya Mansku and Nagahasti. There are quite a few commentaries on these two monumental treasures—Satkhandagama and Kasayapahuda. The last of the commentaries on *Sadkhandagama* called *Dhavala* is by Virasetia, which comprises 72 thousand verses. The commentary on Kasaya pahuda, called *Jayadhavala* is equally monumental having 20 thousand verses written by Virasena and 40 thousand added by his disciple Jinasena. The final portion of the Satkhandagama is called *Mahabandha* which has 41 thousand verses. This has been composed by Bhutabali himself. Fortunately, all those three monumental Agamas are treasured at Mudabidri's temple library. Acharya Nemi Chand Sidhanta Sastri Chakravarti of the last century was supposed to be an authority on these three Agamas. He had composed *Gommatsara* and *Labdhisara* to give the essences of these Agamas. Todarmal has written commentaries upon Gommatsara and Labdhisara in Bhasa. Acharya Kundakunda's *Samayasara, Pravachana-sara, Niyamsara* and *Pancha-stikaya* sara are in acknowledged Prakrit works which are regarded as good as the Agamas by the Jainas. Kundakunda's disciple Umaswati wrote Tattvartha Suttra; which is regarded as the Veritable Bible of the Jainas by both the sects. The legend of the propagation of Jaina religion rests with the Tirthankars and their disciples called eleven Ganadharas who are said to have converted a community of 4411 Sramanas[12] from whom the entire Jaina community have grown.

2. The Contribution of the Agamas

(a) The Validity of Scriptural Knowledge : Except the Charvakas, all systems of Indian Philosophy admit the validity of scriptural knowledge. In the Vedic tradition, the Vedas, which are regarded as impersonal, constitute the highest authority of religion. In the tradition of Sramanic culture of Buddhism and Jainism, the authority of Scriptures rests with their prophets, who are supposed to be Omniscient as well above all *desires and aversions*. In the Jaina tradition, the validity of the scripture is accorded at par with direct perception[13] since the scriptural knowledge is knowledge gained by the Omniscient being, who has directly perceived the reality. Thus scriptural knowledge is also definite, and indubious like the omniscient knowledge. This is admitted by Samantabhadra in his *Apta-Mimansa.*[14] It should also be noted that the knowledge and practice of Scriptures (Agamas) also leads to the attainment of Kevala Jnana, so as to the knower of the Srutas are called *Surta-Kevalin.* Anybody and everybody cannot be Sruta. In order to be a Sruta, he must fulfil the conditions of becoming desireless (*Vitaraga*) and he must destroy the Karmas which obscure the real nature of Sruta.[15] Only then, such a Scriptural knowledge serves like the bliss.[16]

According to the Vedic tradition, the Vedas manifest their own validity. Words used by us, according to them, denote things that can be cognised by other means of knowledge, and, if we cannot know them through other means, then those who utter them must be of unquestionable authority. So non-Vedic utterances cannot possess any inherent validity.[17] According to Prabhakara, such non-Vedic verbal knowledge is of the nature of inference because only the verbal cognition of the Vedas is strictly verbal.[18] The Vedic thinkers adopt the doctrine of impersonate authorship perhaps to maintain its infallibility,[19] because a person is liable to many defects. However, in order to prove the impersonal authorship of the Vedas, the Vedic thinkers; especially the Mimamsakas introduce a mystical theory of the eternality of the Vedas. They hold that the relationship between the word and its meaning is natural and not created by convention. The purpose of the Mimansakas in rejecting the authorship of the Vedas to Gods is because God, who is incorporal, has no organs of speech and hence he cannot utter words, and if He assumes the human form, then He is subject to all the limitations of material existence and hence his utterances will not be authoritative. Then there is no tradition of divine or human authorship of the Vedas. If it is said that the Vedas are human compositions because names of saints and seers occur, it may be said that the hymns deal with the eternal phenomena of nature and the names of persons have only symbolical significance and not any historical significance.

In tracing their Agamas to the utterances of Lord Mahavira, the Jainas have a more secured position. Firstly, since Mahavira is Omniscient (Kevalin) what he says must be true. Since, he is above desires (vitaraga), what he says is free from any subjective prejudices. Lastly, since he is compassionate, what he says is for the benefit of the people. Thus the Jaina theory of scripture as the sermons of Lord Mahavira is more intelligible and rational. The adherence of one's faith in the personality of Lord Mahavira gives a religious colour lastly, such a theory of scripture having its source in the personality of a realised man raises the dignity and status of man to the status of God. Omniscience is not divine but human. It requires a *sadhana.* Thus the Jaina doctrine of Agamas set up everything in real and historical context, while the explanation of the

Impersonality of the Vedas is rather vague and ambiguous. However, it looses at one place—By treating the Vedic authorship as impersonal, it implies that it is perhaps very-very old and ancient because a person is after all a historical event. Here the Jaina reply is that since the truth contained in the Agamas are one, eternal and permanent, it is as old as anything. The objects of the knowledge are the one and the same for all. Hence their cognition is neither new nor old. Hence, there is an argument in the teaching of all the Arhatas.[20] In this sense, the teachings are eternal and universal and hence impersonal. Thus, the line of demarcation between personal and impersonal authorship of the scripture gives way to a reconciliation. A prophetic utterance, in the sense, it is eternal and universal, is impersonal; however, since it comes from the mouth of a historical person, it is personal.

Agama and Its Interpretation : The statement of a trustworthy person is said to be Agama. Otherwise, words themselves are inert, lifeless and even ambiguous. Hence, the validity of *Sabda* rests with the person who uses them. Hence, the interpretation of the Agamas depend both upon the *Speaker* and also upon the *audience.* So far, the speakership of the Jaina Agamas is concerned, it is held to be the direct sermons of the Omniscient Lord, which have been compiled and codified by their chief disciples called Ganadhara[21]. So far the interpretation of the Agamas from the point of view of the audience is concerned, it should be clearly noted that a certain amount of intellectual ability and moral preparation is needed for the appropriate grasp of the subject matter. In absence of such a preparation, the same Agama admits of different and even conflicting interpretations about one and the same subject, like the different interpretations of the *Brahma-Suttra* and the *Bhagavad Gita.* The Jaina Agamas are the sermons of the Tirthankaras which have been correctly reported by the *Sruta-Kevalin* and the *Ganadhara,* who are also supposed to be omniscient and also above all desires of love and hate, hence the validity of the Jaina Agamas is doubly raised because both the *Source* as well as the *Course* of the Agamas are pure.

The Place of Samyika : There are three distinctive contributions of Jainism to Indian Culture-Equality (Sama), Self-control (Sama) and dignity of labour (Srama).[22] Equality or *Samayeya* is said to be the heart of Jainism. In the Jaina religious scripture, *Dvadasangi* or in the 14th Purva,[23] the place of *Samayika* is the first and foremost among the six daily duties. Without the practice of *Samayika* or equality, there is no hope for any religious or spiritual realisation. When a householder accepts the Jaina religion, he solemnly pledges to abide by the principle of equality[24]. The whole of *Visesavasyaka-bhasya* of Jinabhadra Gani is an exposition of this principle of *Samayi*. The three jewels of Jainism, *i.e.* Right Faith, Right Knowledge and Right Conduct[25] depend upon the principle of equality. The Gita calls it the inner poise or the evenness of mind (Samatvam)[26]; or equal mindedness (*Sama Chitatvam*[27] or *Samata*[28]) *and* such a man who attains this is called seer with an equal eye (Sama-darsinah[29] or Sarvatra Sama darsana)[30] This principle of equality must be reflected both in *thought* and *action*. In thought it is the principle of *Anekanta,* in action, it is the principle of *Ahimsa*.

Anekanta : Anekanta is the application of the principle of equality in the sphere of thought. Thus it is not a philosophy but a philosophical standpoint just as there is the Advaitic standpoint of Sankara and the standpoint of the Middle Path of the Buddhists. *Anekanta* literally means non-absolution. Though the Anekanta Period in Jaina philosophical literature comes after the end of the Agamic period, the genesis of the Anekantic idea is already present in the Agamic literature. The famous *Bhagavati Suttra* refers to the important and interesting dreams that Lord Mahavira had just before he had attained Keval Jnana. In one of the dreams, there is reference to "multi-faced" or "multi-coloured" (chitra-vichitra[31]) wings of Pansakholi which Symbolises the multi-faced reality.

The Buddhists also have their doctrine of Vobhajyavada or "conditional expressions", which means that they discard one-sided view (*ekansavada*).[32] However, the Buddhists believed in *Vibhajyavada* to a limited extent, where as the Jainas believe it to the full extent, so that it was finally developed into the Theory of Non-absolutism (*Anekanta vada*).[33] In, Buddhism, *Vibhajya* means *division* and *Vibhajya-Vyakarniya* means "answering a question by dividing." While the Buddhists attribute the divergent attributes at the same time with regard to two different things, the genius of the Jainas is reflected in attributing the different attributes in the one and the same subject, of course, the contexts are different. This leads to the organon of *Sapta-bhangi* and the multivalued logic of Syadvada. Even in the Vedas[34] and Upanisads[35], the description of the reality is in terms of contradictory attributes, like *real and unreal, mobile and immobile.* Nasidiya Sukta therefore, avoids to describe the reality either *as real or unreal.*[36] Thus Anekanta seems to be a dynamic of thought-reconciliation, through which we find an attempt at synthesis between apparently contradictory attributes of eternality and non-eternality of the world[37] or finiteness or infiniteness of the Jiva[38] or difference or non-difference between the body and the soul.[39] Anekanta, however, should not be understood to mean that reality is contradictory. It simply means that it has innumerable number of aspects and attributes which can be thoroughly comprehended only when we can put all of them together. This is ideal of perfection, which can be attained only when we become an omniscient. However, we can have the knowledge of one or other aspect if we are free from prejudice and bias. Thus, on the one hand it has its ideal of finality of knowledge, in reality it aims at aspectal knowledge or *naya*. As a corollary, we have to be cautious in our speech. Lord Mahavira explained every problem with the help of *Siyavaya* or Syadvada.[41] Absolutism in speech and language is as bad as absolutism in thought. The Agamic stress on Anekant and Syadvad is due to its great adherence to Ahimsa. Anekantvada or Syadvada is extension of the principle of Ahimsa on intellectual level. Jainas think that without nonviolence in thought, non-violence in practice is impossible.

Ahimsa : Ahimsa follows as a logical corollary from the principle of Equality (Samya) of souls. The inequalities of physical and mental abilities are only accidental and they are due to the Karmas. How, since "life is dear to all and since everything has got life", we have to accept the principle of Ahimsa as an important means of spiritual realisation. To the Sramanic cult of Jainism, the means are as important as the ends. Our end is no doubt self-realisation or Moksa. Now, this self-realisation is impossible without the love of self and this love of self is nothing other than *Ahimsa,* since self resides in everything. Jainism looks upon the whole world as filled with life. Nothing is fallow or sterile, nothing is dead and inert. What to speak of living beings, even plants and every portion of matter have got life. Hence, respect for life is a spiritual act, it is a law of our being. If we forget it, life becomes well nigh impossible." As we feel our pain, so we must feel the pain of others" says the Acharanga. The same truth is stated in Dasvaikalika where it is clearly said that "all beings desire to live, none want to die". All our religions accept Ahimsa as a virtue but Jainas have worked out a complete philosophy of non-violence, hence here Ahimsa is more due to rational consideration than emotional as we find in Buddhism and Christianity. The Jaina Ahimsa, therefore, embraced the whole universe and is not restricted to humanity. There we can find that Advaita Vedanta and others admit oneness of soul and practically removes the ground of mistrust and violence, which are the result of duality.

Nivarttak Dharma : *Ahimsa* together with *Aparigraha* constitute the ethical wholeness of self-control or self-restraint in social relationship, self-control is the foundation of a higher moral life as in individual life, it is the basis of higher spiritual life. Except for the Mimamsakas, who believe in heaven etc. all the Vaidic and non-Vaidic systems adopt Moksa as the sumnum Bonum of life—which is a state of cessation of the wheels of existence. It is happiness (*Sreya*) rather than pleasure (*preya*) which is the goal of life. Thus self-purification (*atma-suddhi*) and not the acquisition of any earthly or heavenly pleasures, which is the aim of life. The obstacles in the way in the forms of delusion, ignorance and craving must be rooted out by practising the different vows or *Vratas,* throughout life. Hence, the importance of a realised soul rather than some mysterious agency is emphasised. In short, all these constitute the *Nivartaka Dharma* or world-withdrawing religion, which is said to be the heart of Jainism. It is bound to be individualistic, world-withdrawing and self-negating Emphasis on renunciation, asceticism, penances etc. in the account of Sadhana given in the Acharanga is literally soul-stirring, like Buddha, Mahavira also presented a gloomy picture of the world "The living world is afflicted, miserable"—thus begins the second lecture of the first book of *Acharanga.*

"Though a man can conquer thousands and thousands of valient foes, yet greater will be his victory, if he conquers no body but himself."

REFERENCES

1. *Bhagvati Sutra,* V. 54.
2. *Prajna Pana Suttra,* I.
3. Chulla-Vagga-Khuddaka-Vatthu-Khandha-Buddha-Vachana-Nivrtti.
4. *Na Mlecchaitavai Napabhasitavai-Mahabhasya* of Patanjali, p. 49.
5. Sukhalal Sanghvi, *Darsana Aur Chintana* (Ahmedabad, 1957), p. 362.
6. Kailasa Chandra Sastri, *Joint Dharma,* (Kasi 2475 V N), p. 254.
7. Mahendra Kumar Acharya, *Jaina Darsana* (Kasi, 1955 A.D), p. 16 He says that *Harivansa Purana, Jayadhavala, Adi* Parana and Srutavatara also support it. See *Preface* to Jayadhavala, Volume I, pp 47-50.
8. *Dalsukha Malvania, Jaina Darsnika Sahitya Ka Vikas ki Rooprekha* (*Varanasi,* 1952, pp. 1-4).
9. Dalsukha Malvania, *Jaina Darsnika Sahitya Ka Singhavalokana* (Kasi, 1949) pp. 2-3.
10. Dalsukha Malvania, *Jaina Darsnika Sahitya,* p. 6.
11. Kailash Chandra, *Ibid.,* p. 255.
12. *Kalpa-Suttra,* pp. 285.

13. *Gommatsara,* (Jiva-Kanda), Gatha—368 *Tattvartha-Sloka-Varttika,* 1-9-20.
14. *Apta-Mimamsa,* Sloka, 105.
15. *Tattvartha-Sloka-Vartika,* I. 20'2.
16. Kundakunda, *Dasan Pahuda,* Gatha, 17.
17. Parthasarthi Misra, *Sastra-dipika,* p. 53.
18. Salikanah, *Prakrana-Panchika,* p. 88.
19. Kumarila Bhatta, *Sloka-Varttika,* II.
20. *Acharanga-Suttra,* 4. 125, *Sutta-krtanga,* 2.1.15; 2.2.41.
21. *Avasayake-Niryukti,* G. 192 & *Nandi-Suttra,* G. 40.
22. Sukhlal Sanghvi, *Jaina Dharma ka Prana* (Kasi, 1952) p. 2.
23. This is called the *Acharanga Suttra.*
24. *Karemi Bhante Samayeam.*
25. Umaswami, *Tattvartha Sutra* I.I.
26. *Bhagavad Gita,* II. 48.
27. *Ibid.,* XIII. 9.
28. *Ibid.,* X. 5.
29. *Ibid.,* V. 18.
30. *Ibid.,* VI. 29.
31. *Bhagavati Suttra.* 16.6.
32. *Digha-Nikaya,* Sangeet Parinam Suttra No. 33.
33. *Suttra-Krtanga,* I.14.19; I.14.22'. Bhagavati Suttra 7.2.270; 12.2.443; 25.4; 1.8.72.
34. *Rg. Veda,* I.164.46.
35. *Isa-Up.* 5; *Tail Up.* II 7; *Brahad, I,* 21.1; *Chand. Up.* 6.2.
36. *Rg. Veda, X.* 129.
37. *Bhagavati-Suttra,* II. 1; IX. 6; Suttra Krtanga, 1.4.6.
38. *Bhagvati-Suttra* II.1.90; IX.38.7; XIII. 4.481.
39. *Bhagvati-Suttra,* XIII, 7.495; XVII. 2.
40. *Bhagvati-Suttra,* VII. 2.273.
41. Sukhalal Sanghvi, *Jaina-Dharma-Ka-Prana,* p. 2.

13

The Jaina View of Life

Life is a struggle for perfection. Philosophy should serve as the light house in this struggle of life. Hence, true philosophy, must be a philosophy of life. Our attention has uptill now been mainly directed towards the problems of *reality* and *knowledge, God* and *Soul,* etc., but we have neglected *Man.* However, arts and science, philosophy and culture have got significance only in relation to man. Hence, Vyasa correctly said. "There is nothing higher than man" (*nahi sresthataram kimchit manusat*)". Chandidas perhaps went a little further : "Man is higher than everything and nothing is more important than him." (*Sabar upare manusa satya, tahar uppare nai*). Even the Greek Sophists with their own interpretation regarded "man as the measure of all" (*Homo men sura*). The Jainas, even denied God, because they believed in the potential divinity of man. This reminds us of the famous Vedic saying : "Those who know Brahman in Man knows the Being who is Supreme." (*Ye puruse Brahma Viduste Viduh Pasamesthinam-Atharva* Veda, X. VII. 17)

According to Jainism, man can attain divinity contained in the concept of Four-fold Infinities (*anantacatustaya*). Thus it shifted the emphasis from God to Man—an outcome of the development of inwardness. Hence, the interest of Jainism has been centred mainly around man, his morality and destiny. Of the seven fundamental categories of jain philosophy, only two, the 'self' and the 'Non-self' are dealt with from a metaphysical point of view; the other five are more corrolaries-*Asrava* (inflow of karmic-matter) is the cause of mundane existence and

Samvara is the cause of liberation. Everything else is only its amplification.

Our conduct cannot be isolated from our way of life. Truth and valuation are inseperable. Samantabhadra in his *Yuktyanusasanam* (Verse, is) says : "Without knowing the real nature of things, all moral distinctions between bondage and liberation, merit and demerit, pleasure and pain will be blurred."

For Plato, Sanskara and Bradley, philosophy, broadly, is the 'knowledge of reality, for the logical positivist it is only 'linguistic analysis'. However philosophy, to be true, must be philosophy of life, where we do not have a part-view but the whole-view or world-view." Idealism was unable to see the trees in the wood, while empiricism could not see the wood in the trees" said C. D. Broad (*Contemporary British Philosophy*. Ed. J. H. Muirhead, Vol. 1, 1924). These are the two different ways of approaching the problem but they are not the only ways. Hence, we should see the world steadily and as a whole. If we do not look at the world synoptically, we shall have a very narrow view of it. Purely critical philosophy is arid and rigid.

The Jaina view of life known as *anekanta* (Non-absolutism) is nearer to such a synoptic view. To quote Whitehead, such an non-absolutistic approach is "an endeavour to frame a coherent, logical, necessary system of general ideas in terms of which every element of our experience can be interpreted." (A. N. White head : *Process and Reality,* 1929, p. 4). The function of philosophy is not merely academic pursuit of knowledge and reality, it also serves as a way of life. It has the dual purpose of revealing truth and increasing virtue so that it may provide a principle to live by and purposes to live for. Hence, C.E.M. Joad opinions that "We must achieve a synoptic view of the universe". (C.E.M. Joad : A Critique of *Logical Positivism,* 1950, p. 29).

The Jaina attitude of non-absolutism is rooted in its attitude towards life. Life is dear to all. To do harm to others is to do harm to oneself. The *Acharanga Sutra* (1.5.5) declares : ""Thou art he whom thou intendest to tyrannise over." Hence a feeling of immense respect and responsibility for human personàlity inspires Jainism. It has upheld the worth of life very much, hence its main emphasis is on Ahimsa or non-violence.

However its concern for non-violence is more due to ideological consciousness than emotional compassion. Unlike Buddhism, Jainism does not view life a transient and illusory phenomenon, nor it regards it as immutable like the Upanisad-Vedanta philosophers. Infact, both absolute permanence and absolute impermanence is absolute non-sense. Adhering to the common experience, Jainism regards the nature of reality as having the characteristics of origination, decay and continuance—giving a non-exclusivists view.

Secondly, Jainism believes in the potential divinity of man. Given freedom of development, every individual can attain the supreme spiritual progress. Hence, any interference means spiritual degeneration. Violence is nothing but interference with life, hence it must be eschewed in thought, word and deed. In this context, Anekantavada (non-absolutism) is an extension of Ahimsa in the realm of thought and so is Syadvada a logical corollary in the field of speech. Anything should be viewed not from only one standpoint (*ekanta*) but from many angles of vision. The real is a variable constant, hence there must be variable angles of vision, which will negate dogmatism and imperialism of thought. 'Ekanta', means the 'only' point of view, whereas *Anekant* implies the principle of reciprocity and interaction among the reals of the universe.

This Anekant-ideology is the spirit of synthesis (*Samanvya-drsti*) nutured into the synthetic culture of India. In the Vedas and Upanisads, the ultimate reality is described neither as real (Sat) nor as unreal (Asat). Some described the reality as one, while others hold it as many. In fact, the ultimate reality is the same, though it is called by different names. Aynanvada or Agnesticism of Canjaya shows reconciliatory spirit through his Four-fold or Five-fold formula of denial so the Vibhayavada or the Critical method of Investigation of Buddha is contrasted with the *Ekantavada*. This is his doctrine of Middle Path or the Madhym-pratipada which induced Buddha to "treat prevalent opinions with all due consideration." Nagarjuna's Diabeties of Fourfold Antinomies (*catuskoti*) resembles Anekanta approach. The *Bhedabheda* system of Bharataprapancha is actually referred to as Anekanta. While the Bhatta Mimamsa and the Samkhya have an anekanta bias with respect to some of their ideas and methods. Therefore, Santarakshita attributes the concept of vaicitrya to the Mimamsa as well to the Sankhyas. Even the critique on the light doctrines of Gautama resemble the Anekantavada in its spirit and form although they are not as pervasive as they are in Jainism.

Anekantavada is the heart of Jainism. It constitutes its moral original contribution to the philosophical speculation. However, Anekantavad-syadvada has been more maligned than understood even by the great Vedantic and Buddhist Acharyas. It is misfortune that system like Advaita which realises the inadequacy of logic to appreciate the evidence of experience as well as the probablistic interpretation of multi-valued logics, which can reconcile the apparent contradictions in the Anekantavada. Anekanta implies twin functions of analysis and synthesis known as conjunctive and disjunctive diabetics respectively or Nayavada and Syadvada.

Viewed in the light of the doctrine of Anekanta, the reality reveals not merely as any (anantatmakam) but also as infinitely manifold (*ananta-dharmatmam-kam*). The reality is possessed of infinite number of attributes and human knowledge is limited untill it attains omniscience. Hence we cannot have the complete grasp of the whole reality or an absolute affirmation or complete negation of a predicate. To know is to relate, therefore our knowledge is essentially relative and limited in many ways. In the sphere of application of the means of knowledge or in the extent of the knowable our thought is relative. The whole reality in its completeness, cannot be grasped by this partial thought. The objectivity of the universe reveals that the universe is independent of the mind which implies principle of distinction leading to the recognition of non-absolutism.

In absolute sense, a thing is neither real nor unreal, neither permanent not evanscent but both. This dual nature of things is proved by a reductio-ad-absurdum of absolutism. Further, this is also the basis of the Law of Causation, because an 'absolute real' can neither be cause nor an effect. However, an 'absolute flax' cannot be the basis of operation for the Law of Causation. Similarly, the controversy between unity and pharality can be easily solved by the Anekanta logic, which affirms attributes in a unitary entity. A thing is neither an absolute unity nor an irreconciliable multiplicity. Infact, it is both multiplicity-in-unity. Similarly, both absolute existence and non-existence are metaphysical abstractions.

To say that a thing is neither real or unreal, neither eternal not non-eternal, neither static nor mobile but partakes of the dual nature perhaps is an affront to the believers in the traditional Laws of thought. No body rejects them but these abstract fomulations are not suited to dynamic character of the universe. Our own observation and experience reveals that the two-valued logic seems to be unreal. So far that abstract formulation of the Laws of Thought A is A Identity, A is not A (contradiction). A is either A or not A (Excluded Midoh). They may be right. But their concrete formulations (A Radio is a Radio) admits of change. A real radio is constantly under going change hence there is change according to space and time. Similarly, even change is meaningless without the idea of persistence. Hence the contradiction (A Skylab cannot both be and not be) is only national because 'A Skylab' is a Skylab so long it works as a laboratory in the Sky but when it takes as a debris after degeneration, if it is not the same sky-lab in the same condition. Hence, a skylab can be both a skylab and not a skylab. There is no difficulty to accept this in actual experience.

The denial of pre-non-existence and past-non-existence as part of a real leads to the impossibility of all theoretical and practical activily. Similarly, the denial of non-existence of mutual identity (numerical differences) and absolute non-existence is also impossible. If there is no difference, there will be no distinction, hence no independence between subject and object. If there is negation of identity, there is worse confusion. Hence the nature of reality can neither be exclusively *identity* nor *multiplicity*. As regards relations, no relation is meaningful if there is pure identity and no relation is possible between the two absolutely independent and different terms. Similarly regarding causal efficiency, the real cannot be either 'absolute constant' nor can it be an 'absolute variant' but a "variable constant."

It is asked, whether this kind of non-absolutism is itself *absolute* or *not*. If it is former, there is at least one real which is absolute; if it is not, it is not absolute and universal fact. Whether non-absolutism is itself absolute or relative depends upon the nature of proposition which is either complete (Sakladesa) or incomplete (Vikladesa). The former being the object of valid knowledge (Pramana) and the latter, two object of aspectal knowledge (naya), This means that the directive of non-absolutism is not absolute unconditionally. However, to avoid the fallacy of infinite regress, the Jainas distinguish between true the non-absolutism (Samyaka-Anekanta) and false non-absolutism (Mithya-Anekanta). To be valid, therefore, non-absolutism must not be *absolute* but always *relative*. When one attribute is stated as constitution the whole nature of the real and thus implies the negation of other attributes, such cognitions are examples of the 'false absolute.' But *Naya* is not false though it is partial or knowledge from a particular standpoint.

The nature of unconditionality in the statement "All statements are conditional" is quite different from the normal meaning of unconditionality. This is like the idea contained in the passage "I do not know myself" where there is no contradiction between *knowledge* and *ignorance*, or in the statement 'I am undecided', where there is atleast one decision : "I am undecided" the unconditionality is not at the level of existence, while at the level of *essence* (thought) anything is alternative. We do not live in the realm of *thought* or *reason* above. Behind *reason,* there is always the watershed of *unreason* or *faith.* The Jainas, too have faith in their scriptures as anybody else has in his or her. Her is unconditionally. In each community, there is a special absolute. The absolutes themselves are alternation so far as they are possible (till we are on thought level), but I have chosen one and stick to it, it is more than possible, it is existent or actual. At this point, there may be a reconciliation between conditionality and unconditionality. On thought level, the statement "Everything is conditional", holds good but when we adopt the point of view of *existence,* we are led to rest with unconditionality.

Ideologically, we cannot make one-sided exposition. But in actual usage, whenever we make any particular statement (S is P or S is not P), it takes the form of a categorical proposition. Even a Hypothetical (If S then P) or a Disjunctive (Either S or P) is said to have a categoric basis and therefore, they can be converted into categorical propositions. But since our thought is relative, so must be our expression.

There is another problem also—how to synthesise the different angles of visions or internal harmony of the opposed predications (S is P, S is not P, S is both P and not P; S is neither P nor not P). It *is,* therefore, the Jainas prefix *Syat* (Somehow, in some respect) as a corrective against any absolutist way of thought and evaluation of reality. This is a linguistic tool for the practical application of non-absolutism in words. Because of this prefix *Syat* and the relative nature of proposition, it is called *Syadvada,* But words are only expressive or suggestive (Vachaka or Jnapaka) rather than productive (Karaka). Thus the meaning is, however, eventually rooted in nature of things in reality and we have, therefore, to explore a scheme of linguistic symbols (*Vachanvinyasa*) for model judgements representing alternate standpoints. (*Nayas*), or a way of approach or a particular opinion (*abhipraya*), or view-point (*apekasa*).

This philosophy of standpoints bears the same relation to philosophy as logic does to thought or grammer to language. We cannot affirm or deny anything absolutely of any object owing to the endless complicity of things, Every statement of a thing, therefore, is bound to be one-sided and incomplete. Hence the doctrine of seven Fold predication (Saptaphang) in the logical consumption *at* the doctrine of relative standpoints (*Syadvada*). If we insist on absolute predication without conditions (Syat), the only cause open is to dismiss either the diversity or the identity as a mere metaphysical fiction. Every single standpoint designated in every statement has a partial truth. Different aspects of reality can be considered from different perspectives (*Nikshopa*). Thus Naya is the analytic and Saptabhang is the synthetic method of studying ontological problems.

If this form of statements, this doctrine insists on the correlation of affirmation and negation. All judgements are double-edged in character-existent and non-existent. The predicate of inexpressibility stands for the unique synthesis of existence and non-existence and is therefore 'unspeakable' (avakatavya). Thus three predicates—'existence', 'non-existence' and 'inexpressibility' make seven exhaustive and unique modes of expression of truth.

We are aware of various criticisms against Anekantavad-Syadvad, that they involve the Fallacies of self-contradiction (Virodha). Absence of Common Abodi (*Vaiyadhikaranya*) Infinite Regress (Anavastha) Confusion (Sankara) exchange of Natures (*Vyatikara*), Doubt (Samsaya), Non-apprehension (*Apratipatti*), Both sides (Ubhaya) etc. However, we do not want to go into details.

We have considered the most formidable criticism that how far non-obsolutism of Syadvada is not absolute but relative. However, it is wrong to confuse the Pragmatic and Pluralistic realistic attitude of syadvada with either Pragmatism of James-Diway-either or with the *objective relativism* of the sophists or even with the *relative absolutism* of Whitehead or

Bodis or with Eeinstinician relativity except in the most general attitude. Pyrroh's prefixing every judgement with a 'may be' must not be identifical Jaina 'Syat'. The former degenerates into Agnesticism or Scepticism, the latter leaves no room for any such thing. Scepticism means in the minimum, absence of any assertion, whereas Syadvadins always assert, though what they assert are alternatives—each being valied in its own Universe of Discourse, which controls the interpretation of everyword. This is the logic of Relatives.

Perhaps on account of its cathalicity of outlook, Syadvada is branded as a form 'eclecticism' or a 'philosophy of compromise' "Since an eclectic system is a loose piece of mosaic work, rather than an organised body of original thought, the term has come to be one of reproach". However, this is unjust to brand it as a "loose piece of mosaic work" or "odd collection of arbitrary half-truths". In fact the truths presented are alternative truths which are true in their own aspects. Of course, Syadvada rejects the 'dispotic absolute truth' or the 'block universe' or a 'seemless coat'. Even in the synthesis achieved through the dynamics of Syadvada, there is 'discriminative unity' rather than 'secondless unit'. In short, absolutism in thought is rejected to avoid arbitrariness in action.

To brand Syadvada as *agnesticism* or Scepticism like that of *Sanjaya* or of Pyrroho is again another injustice. The prefix 'Syat' does not mean 'perhaps' but 'in respect of' a particular context. Each model truth is valid from its own standpoint. It is not a doctrine of "know nothingness" or "unknowability". Each standpoint of the saptbhangi is definite in its own place. Syadvada statements are not "indefinite" (Belvalkar). But "indeterminate" (Hiriyanna) which means that it cannot be defined absolutely. No single mode of expression is adequate to express the nature of reality. The various modes of truths are not merely many truths, but alternative truths, each being as definite as anything.

Regarding the charge of "Self-contradiction" against Syadvada by the great Vedantic and Buddhistic Acharyas, I feel that the motive behind it must be extra-logical. How one can believe that Dharmakirti will call Anekantvada as mere non-sensical talk (Pralapmatra) in view of Jaina theory of dual character of universal and particular of a thing. He asks of all realities are Sat, there would be no difference between *cow* and *camel.* Pragnakara Gupta and Archat point out that the triple charactered nature of reality having origination, destruction and permanence cannot exist together and hence is self contradictory. Santarakshita thinks that there would be a commingling (*Sankarya*) and a confusion (*Sandha*) in the dual nature of reality, the result of which would not be helpful to decide which is general and which particular.

Karnakagomin also refutes the dual characteristic theory of the Jainas in his own way. In his famous treatise Refutation of Anekantvada (Anekantavada Nirasa), Jitari says that one cannot have identity as well as difference by the same nature.

Sankar and Ramanya also point out to the violation of the law of contradiction.

However, all these thinkers forget that the laws of thoughts should be considered by the testimony of experience and not be pre-conception. Experience shows that a thing is real in own respect but not so in other respect.

The triple character theory is supported through *anvathanupapannatava hetu.* Prom the realistic standpoint there is no such difference which could indicate the separation between identity and difference. The reality is synthism of identity-in difference and each synthesis is a Jatyautara (Sui generis). Aklanka points out that the Buddhists philosophers ignore the formula Sarvobhavstudatasvabhati and tries to establish equality between curd and camel.

Infact, Syadvada is against the formulations of formal two-valued logic. It avoids vicious intellectualism and the fallacy of exclusive particularity. Thus Syadavad is a new dynamics of thinking which is based on cathokicism and regard for truth seen from different angles.

Index

T

U

W

Y